T0055648

CHARTS OF

BIBLE
PROPHECY

Books in the Zondervan*Charts* Series

CHARTS OF

BIBLE PROPHECY

H. Wayne House

ZONDERVAN™
GRAND RAPIDS, MICHIGAN 49530 USA

ZONDERVAN

Charts of Bible Prophecy
Copyright © 2003 by H. Wayne House and World of the Bible Ministries, Inc.

Requests for information should be addressed to:
Zondervan, *Grand Rapids, Michigan 49530*

Library of Congress Cataloging-in-Publication Data

House, H. Wayne
    Charts of bible prophecy / H. Wayne House and Randall Price — 1st. ed.
      p. cm. — (Zondervan Charts)
    ISBN 978-0-310-21896-8
    1. Bible—Prophecies I. Price, Randall. II. Title. III. Series.
  BS647.3.H68 2003
  dc21
                                                          2003019757

Permission to use or adapt previously published material is indicated on the Acknowledgments page, which hereby becomes a part of this copyright page.

All Scripture quotations, unless otherwise noted, are taken from the *Holy Bible: New International Version*®. Copyright © 1973, 1978, 1984 by International Bible Society. Used by permission of Zondervan. All rights reserved.

Scripture quotations marked NASB are taken from the *New American Standard Bible*®, © Copyright 1960, 1962, 1963, 1968, 1971, 1972, 1973, 1975, 1977 by The Lockman Foundation. Used by permission.

Scripture quotations marked NKJV are taken from the *New King James Version*. Copyright © 1982 by Thomas Nelson, Inc. Used by permission. All rights reserved.

All rights reserved. No part of this publication may be reproduced, stored in a retrieval system, or transmitted in any form or by any means — electronic, mechanical, photocopy, recording, or any other — except for brief quotations in printed reviews, without the prior permission of the publisher.

Interior design by Sherri L. Hoffman
Interior illustrations by Joel and Kimberly Tovolacci, and www.arttoday.com

Printed in the United States of America

To my wife, Beverlee,
with whom I look joyfully to the future.

Randall Price

In memory of my parents, Joseph Walter
and Sarah Oma Ellen House, and my brothers,
James and David House. They have gone before me,
but I rejoice and look for the first resurrection
(1 Thess. 4:13–18), over which death
has no more power (Rev. 20:6).

H. Wayne House

Contents

Preface

The study of biblical prophecy is one of the great endeavors of the Christian life. In fact, to study the Bible itself is to study prophecy, because when it was first written, the greater percentage of its message was yet unfulfilled. Today the church stands between the comings of Christ. We look backward for our beginning to Christ's first coming and the cross and look forward to Christ's second coming and the crown.

The concept of the second coming of Christ is found some 1,845 times in the Old Testament and 318 times in the New Testament. In the former it is the dominant theme of 17 books, and in the latter every book but 3 includes this teaching, as does the whole book of Revelation. To bring these statistics home, in the New Testament this means an average of 7 out of 10 chapters or 1 in every 12 verses (1 in 10 in the Epistles). This reminds us that God is very much interested in our knowing what he has planned for this world and for our lives in the future.

Within the church, different systems of interpretation have arisen over the last 2,000 years to interpret the prophetic scriptures. The view of the Jewish nation and of the early Jewish-Christian church was the futurist school, represented by premillennialism. The view of the predominantly gentile church, especially from the third century, was that of the historicist school, represented by amillennialism, and also the preterist school, represented by postmillennialism. The charts that reflect the viewpoint of the authors of this book present the futurist interpretation (premillennialism) and a later development of it, dispensationalism, which is known as pretribulational premillennialism. Simply put, this school teaches that the next event on the prophetic calendar is the rapture of the church, which will be followed by a period of tribulation, the second advent of Christ, and the establishment of the kingdom of Christ on earth (the millennium). Other charts present the views of the historicist and preterist schools, and especially their common view of Israel's replacement by the church, called replacement theology. While we do not agree with this view, we feel it is important to understand these schools so you can make a proper evaluation in light of Scripture, the ultimate interpreter of all systems.

Most of the charts in this collection have been prepared by the authors, but some are reprinted or adapted from other published works. We are grateful to those who kindly granted use of their materials in special ways. Readers are encouraged to consult their respective works for additional resources.

We trust all these charts will prove useful in your study of the prophetic Word. Our purpose is to help clarify God's Word concerning the ancient context of the Bible—the world of the Bible—and to make its truths relevant today.

Acknowledgments

The authors are grateful to those people and organizations that have granted permission to use charts in whole or in part. Our special thanks go to Dr. Thomas Ice of the Pre-Trib Research Center in Arlington, Texas; Dr. Harold L. Willmington of Liberty Bible Institute in Lynchburg, Virginia; and Dr. Rick Griffith of Singapore Bible College.

The sources are indicated at their respective charts throughout this book. Also, the chart numbers are given in italics after each entry in the lists below.

Permission has been granted to use material from the following sources:

Richard P. Belcher, *A Comparison of Dispensationalism and Covenant Theology* (Columbia, SC: Richbarry Press, n.d.). *45*

Thomas L. Constable, "A Theology of Joshua, Judges, and Ruth," in *A Theology of the Old Testament,* ed. Roy B. Zuck (Chicago: Moody Press, 1991). *10*

Larry Crutchfield, "Israel and the Church in the Ante-Nicene Fathers," part 1 of "Rudiments of Dispensationalism in the Ante-Nicene Period," *Bibliotheca Sacra* 144, no. 575 (July-September 1987). *49*

Larry Crutchfield, "Ages and Dispensations in the Ante-Nicene Fathers," part 2 of "Rudiments of Dispensationalism in the Ante-Nicene Period," *Bibliotheca Sacra* 144, no. 576 (October-December 1987). *47*

Paul Enns, *Moody Handbook of Theology* (Chicago: Moody Press, 1989). *39, 87*

Rick Griffith, *Eschatology: The Study of Future Events,* 7th ed. (Singapore: Singapore Bible College, 1999). *9, 10, 11, 13, 50, 51, 90, 115, 116, 117, 119*

Robert G. Gromacki, *New Testament Survey* (Grand Rapids: Baker Book House, 1974). *94, 105*

John Hannah, "Advances in Dispensationalism" (Unpublished transparency). *41*

Harold W. Hoehner, *Chronological Aspects of the Life of Christ* (Grand Rapids: Zondervan, 1977). *38*

Thomas Ice, *Bible Prophecy Charts* (Arlington, TX: The Pre-Trib Research Center, n.d.). *7, 32, 44, 60, 67*

David Larsen, *Israel, Gentiles, and the Church* (Grand Rapids: Discovery House, 1998). *68*

J. Barton Payne, *Encyclopedia of Biblical Prophecy* (New York: Harper & Row, 1973). *14, 17, 63*

J. Dwight Pentecost, "Daniel," in *The Bible Knowledge Commentary: Old Testament Edition,* ed. John F. Walvoord and Roy B. Zuck (Wheaton, IL: SP Publications, 1985). *23*

Ronald W. Pierce, "Spiritual Failure, Postponement, and Daniel 9," *Trinity Journal,* n.s., 10, no. 2 (Fall 1989). *106*

Charles C. Ryrie, *Dispensationalism Today* (Chicago: Moody Press, 1965). *42*

Harold Willmington, *Prophetic Charts* (Privately published, 1999). *54, 55*

Roy B. Zuck, *Basic Bible Interpretation* (Colorado Springs: Victor Books, 1991). *15*

The authors also drew on material that appears as text and not in chart form in the following sources:

Millard J. Erickson, *Christian Theology,* vol. 3 (Grand Rapids: Baker, 1985). *52, 87*

Terry C. Hulbert, "The Eschatological Significance of Israel's Annual Feasts" (Th.D. dissertation, Dallas Theological Seminary, 1965). *62*

Jewish traditional sources, including Seder Olam, Talmud, Midrash, Rabbah, Commentaries by Rashi, Maimonides, Abarbanel, Targum Onkelos and Jonathan on the Torah, and Targum Jonathan on the Prophets. *16*

Paul S. Karleen, *The Prewrath Rapture of the Church: Is It Biblical?* (Langhorne, PA: BF Press, 1991). *52*

William Hendricksen, *More Than Conquerors* (Grand Rapids: Baker Book House, 1998). *107*

Anthony Hoekema, *The Bible and the Future* (Grand Rapids: William B. Eerdmans, 1986). *87*

Manish Jacob, "A Study of Hindu Eschatology in Comparison with Dispensational Eschatology" (Unpublished research paper for the course TH 304 Eschatology, Singapore Bible College, May 1991). *118*

Raymond Ludwigson, *A Survey of Bible Prophecy* (Grand Rapids: Zondervan, 1973). *80*

Brempong Oswusu-Anti, *The Chronology of Daniel 9:24–27.* Adventist Theological Society Dissertation Series, vol. 2 (Berrien Springs, MI: Adventist Theological Society, 1995). *92*

Marvin Rosenthal, *The Prewrath Rapture of the Church* (Nashville: Thomas Nelson, 1990). *52*

Robert L. Thomas, *Revelation 1–7,* Wycliffe Exegetical Commentary (Chicago: Moody Press, 1992). *103*

Robert L. Thomas, *Revelation 8–22,* Wycliffe Exegetical Commentary (Chicago: Moody Press, 1995). *103*

Ephraim Urbach, *The Sages: Their Concepts and Beliefs* (Cambridge, MA: Harvard University Press, 1987). *16*

John T. Willis, *My Servants the Prophets,* vol. 1 (Abilene, TX: Bible Research Press, 1971). *3*

The following charts were previously published in Wayne House, *Charts of Christian Theology and Doctrine* (Grand Rapids: Zondervan, 1992):

A Comparison of Covenant Theology and Dispensationalism. *45*

Views on the Rapture. *52*

Views on the Millennium. *87*

PART 1

An Introduction to Prophecy

1. Prophecy and Archaeology

Prophetic texts for which archaeological evidence of historical fulfillment exists			
Prophecy	**Biblical Text**	**Historical Fulfillment**	**Archaeological Confirmation**
Jerusalem to be delivered from invasion and siege of Assyrians. Assyrian king Sennacherib to withdraw and return to his own city, never again to attack Jerusalem.	2Ki 19:32-33 ; 2Ch 32:1-23; Isa 37:33-35	Jerusalem spared (701 B.C.) Sennacherib killed (681 B.C.) 2Ki 19:35-37; 2Ch 32:21; Isa 37:36-38	The Taylor Prism records Sennacherib's boast of laying siege to Jerusalem but not its capture. Herodotus records retreat of Assyrian army. Babylonian Chronicle records Sennacherib's assassination.
City of Tyre to be captured by the Babylonians, its island scraped bare like a rock, its stones and timbers thrown into the sea. Tyre to become place where fishermen spread nets, never to be rebuilt.	Eze 26:4-8, 12-14; 28:1-10; Zec 9:3-4	Siege by Nebuchadnezzar (585-572 B.C.) Causeway built by Alexander (332 B.C.)–stones and timbers in sea Final destruction by Muslims in 1291	Babylonian Chronicle, Babylonian court document *The Court of Nebuchadnezzar*, and tablets from the Erech Archive provide details of Babylonian siege. Historical records of Herodotus, Xenophon, and Josephus Flavius (*Antiquities*) provide other details.
Assyrian capital of Nineveh to be destroyed; attackers to have red shields and garments.	Na 2:3-6, 8; 2:13; Zep 2:13-15	Fall of Nineveh to Babylonians (612 B.C.)	Babylonian Chronicle records coalition formed by Babylonian king Nabopolassar and red-painted shields and tunics of the Median and Babylonian armies. Nineveh was left desolate, its location forgotten until discovery in late eigteenth century and again excavated between 1820-46.
Persian king Cyrus specifically named as deliverer of Jews, to destroy Babylon and to serve as instrument for rebuilding Jerusalem temple and returning temple vessels taken by Babylonians.	Isa 41:25; 44:28–45:1; 52:11-12; Jer 27:19-28:6; Da 5:28	Fall of Babylon (539 B.C.) Cyrus decree (538 B.C.) 2Ch 36:22-23; Ezr 1:1-11; Da 5:30-31	Herodotus and Xenophon record Persian army's conquest of Babylon by diverting Euphrates River. Cyrus Cylinder and Xanthos Stela contain similar structure and wording to decree of 538 B.C. and reveal Cyrus's policy for restoring foreign temples.
Jerusalem and the second (Herodian) temple would be destroyed; every stone of the temple mount would be thrown down.	Mt 24:2; Mk 13:2; Lk 21:6, 20-24	Jerusalem and temple destroyed by Roman army under Titus in A.D. 70; description by Josephus Flavius (*Wars*)	Excavations (Jewish Quarter by Avigad, south and west corners of temple mount by Mazar, Ben-Dov, Bahat, and Reich) revealed destruction of city and stones thrown to street level, with no trace of temple structures on platform.

2. Prophetic Statistics

23,210	verses in the Old Testament	7,914	verses in the New Testament
6,641	verses of *prophecy* in Old Testament	1,711	verses of *prophecy* in New Testament
28.6%	*of the Old Testament is prophecy*	21.6%	*of the New Testament is prophecy*

TOTAL

31,124	verses in whole Bible
8,352	verses of biblical prophecy
27%	⅓ of whole Bible is prophecy

EXAMPLE: SECOND COMING OF CHRIST

First prophecy in Bible (Jude 14)

Last prophecy in Bible (Rev 22:20)

found in

1,845 verses in OT (dominant theme of 17 books in OT)

318 verses in NT (in every book but 3)

=7 out of every 10 chapters or 1 out of every 12 verses (10 in Epistles)

3. Prophets and Prophecy

CATEGORIES OF PROPHETS	DESIGNATIONS OF THE PROPHETS
Precanonical Prophets Noah (Heb 11:7; 1Pe 3:20; Ge 9:25-27) Enoch (Jude 14) Abraham (Ge 27) Moses (Hos 12:13; Dt 18:15-22; 34:10) Samuel Elijah Elisha **Canonical Prophets** Writers of the prophetic books of the Hebrew Scriptures. Daniel would be included in this listing though he is found in the third section of the Hebrew canon (the Writings) rather than the section called the Prophets.	**Man of God** (אִישׁ אֱלֹהִים, *ish elohim*) Samuel (1Sa 2:27; 9:6-8, 10); Elijah (1Ki 17:18, 24); Elisha (2Ki 5:8, 14) **Spokesman** (נָבִיא, *nabim*) for Yahweh (Dt 34:10; 2Ki 3:11); for Moses (Ex 7:1) **Seer** (רֹאֶה, *roʾeh*) because of how prophets received their messages (Eze 1:4-28; Zec 1-6); earlier term than *prophet* (1Sa 9:9; cf. 2Sa 24:11; 2Ki 17:13; Isa 29:10; 30:10; Mic 3:6-7; where חֹזֶה, *chozeh,* is used) **Assayer** (בָּחוֹן, *bachon*) one who tests genuineness, like a tester of metal (Jer 6:27) **Servant** (עֶבֶד, *ebed*) of Yahweh (Isa 43:10; 44:26; Jer 7:25; Eze 38:17; Am 3:7) **Messenger** (מַלְאָךְ, *malak*) (2Ch 36:15-16; Isa 44:26; Hag 1:13) **Watchman** (שָׁמַר, *shamar*) (2Sa 18:24-27; Jer 31:6; 51:12); one who warned of impending danger (צָפָה, *tsaphah*) (Jer 6:17; Eze 3:17; 33:2, 6-7; Hos 9:8)

Chart 3—*Prophets and Prophecy (Cont.)*

Message of the Old Testament Prophets
Called their people to return to or remain faithful to Yahweh and his covenant
Fought against the syncretism of Yahwism and Baalism
Anointed the kings of Israel (1Sa 10:1; 16:1, 13; 1Ki 1:34, 39, 45) and rebuked them (2Sa 12:7-12; 1Ki 21:17-24)
Championed the cause of the poor and oppressed (1Sa 12:3-4; 2Sa 12:1-4; 1Ki 17:8-16; 21:17-24; Jer 7)

TESTS FOR TRUE AND FALSE PROPHETS

Unreliable Tests	Partially Reliable Tests	Fully Reliable Tests
The extent of a man's training in religious ministry did not have a necessary relationship to his genuineness (cf. Jer 1:1; Eze 1:3 with Am 7:14-15). Ecstatic experiences by prophets are not necessarily an indication that the prophets are genuine. (1Sa 19:20-24; 2Ki 3:15; Eze 2:2; but cf. 1Ki 18:26-29). Popularity among the people of God was not a sign of a genuine prophet (Jer 23:13-15; cf. 1Ki 22:26-27; Jer 19:14-20:2). A prophet's affirmation that he was speaking God's word did not indicate genuineness (Jer 27:4 with Jer 28:1-2 and 1Ki 22:11). The sincerity of a prophet did not guarantee genuineness (Jer 8:18-9:1 with Jer 23:25-32 and Eze 13:6-7).	Hearers expected a prophet to practice what he preached (Isa 28:7; Jer 23:14; Eze 13:22). However, this was not a sure test of genuineness (cf. Ro 3:23; Jer 38:24-27; Gal 2:11-14). True prophets brought a message of doom to a sinful nation (Jer 28:8; cf. Jer 25:11-12 with Jer 28:2-4). However, true prophets also brought hope for the future (cf. Am 5:14; Jer 30:3; 31:16-20). When a man predicted a future event and it came to pass, he was considered a true prophet (Jer 28:9; 44:26-29; Eze 13:6). If it did not come to pass, he was a false prophet (Dt 18:21-22; Jer. 37:19). However, Dt 13:1-3 says not to believe a prophet whose predictions come true if he advocates worship of other gods. Also Jer 17:15 says people refused Jeremiah because his prophecies had not been fulfilled. All of Jeremiah's listeners would be dead when his prophecies were fulfilled. When a prophet predicted a nation would fall, the fulfillment of the prophecy would occasionally be determined by whether the nation repented or not. (Jer 18:7-8; cf. Jnh 3:4 and 3:5-10; but also the opposite Jer 18:9-10). Prophets were not founders of a new religion and were "Bible" centered (Am 1:3, 6, 9; Jer 6:16; 7:1-3; 28:1-17; 1Ki 22:11-23). However, false prophets used Scripture and agreed with it (cf. Am 3:2; Hos 11:1; Jer 2:13)	The fact that a prophet used Scripture was not a fully reliable test; it was *how* he used Scripture that mattered. The Israelites believed that since God had chosen Israel and since they obeyed even the small details of the law (Isa 1:10-17; Am 4:4-5) that God would not disinherit them, punish them, or let a wicked nation drive them out. The genuine prophets recognized this as a bargain-counter religion. God was a person and demanded personal relationship. False prophets did not apply Scripture correctly. They used Scripture as proof texts to support preconceived ideas. Their messages were irrelevant to the real needs of the people. True prophets recognized that God's choice of Israel meant that Israel had greater responsibility than the nations (Am 3:1-2). Deeds are worthless without heart and life devotion to Yahweh (Isa 1:15; 29:13; Am 5:22-23). There could be little doubt that a prophet was genuine if his message was the direct cause of persecution that he would not otherwise have experienced and yet he did not renounce the message in spite of the consequences (1Ki 22:24-28; Jer 38:1-6).

Much of the above is based on notes from a class with John T. Willis and on his book *My Servants the Prophets*, vol. 1 (Abilene, TX: Biblical Research Press, 1971), 15-21.

4. An Overview of Prophetic Books

Prophet	Date of Ministry	Where Prophet Lived	Where Prophet Ministered	Political Conditions	Spiritual Conditions	Main Message	Reference in Historical Books
Obadiah	845 B.C.	Judah	Judah	Jehoram king	Discouragement	Encouragement for the Jews and indication of Edom's final doom	2Ch 21:16-17
Joel	835 B.C.	Judah	Judah	Elders and priests dominating scene	Indeference and drunkenness	Call for national repentance	2Ki 11
Jonah	782 B.C.	Israel	Israel or Nineveh Prosperous, fearful of growing	Giants in east and west Great wickedness		Destruction of Nineveh	2Ki 14
Hosea	760 B.C.	Israel	Israel	Golden age of prosperity coming to an end	Approaching lowest point of morality	Spiritual adultery of Israel	2Ki 18
Amos	760 B.C.	Judah	Israel	Height of prosperity	Moral corruption	Judgment on Israel	2Ki 14
Isaiah	739 B.C.	Judah	Judah	Assyria in ascendancy	Period of degeneracy and idolatry	God's plan concerning his people	2Ki 15-20 2Ch 26-32
Micah	735 B.C.	Judah	Judah	Assyria in ascendancy	Low	Judgment of Judah and Israel and Messiah's deliverance	2Ki 15,16 2Ch 28
Nahum	650 B.C.	Judah	Northern Captivity Israel	Instability	Period of degeneracy, idolatry, violence, and arrogance	Nineveh will be destroyed by Babylon	None
Zephaniah	640 B.C.	Judah	Northern Captivity Israel	Social injustice	Very low	Day of Yahweh	2Ki 23

PART 1: AN INTRODUCTION TO PROPHECY

Chart 4—An Overview of Prophetic Books (Cont.)

Prophet	Date of Ministry	Where Prophet Lived	Where Prophet Ministered	Political Conditions	Spiritual Conditions	Main Message	Reference in Historical Books
Jeremiah	627 B.C.	Judah	Northern Captivity Israel	Nations jockeying for world power	Complete defection: pagan cults and idolatry rampant	Destruction and restoration	2Ki 22
Habakkuk	609 B.C.	Judah	Northern Captivity Israel	Babylon rising in power	Idolatry rampant	Holiness of God	2Ki 22
Daniel	605 B.C.	Babylon	Southern Captivity Judah	Transition from Babylonian to Persian rule	Discipline and deportation	Sovereignty of God over the nations	2Ki 24
Ezekiel	593 B.C.	Babylon	Southern Captivity Judah	Jews in Babylonian captivity	Under discipline	Restoration	2Ki 24
Haggai	520 B.C.	Judah	Judah	Reforming government and temple	Materialistic	Call for the Jewish remnant to finish the temple	Ezr 5:1
Zechariah	520 B.C.	Babylon and Judah	Judah	Temple not built and country disorganized	Depression	Restoration and cleansing of the nation	Ezr 5; Ne 12
Malachi	433 B.C.	Judah	Judah	Still under foreign yoke but trying to become organized	Cured of idolatry	God condemns the ungodly behavior of his people.	None

5. Parables Relating to Prophecy

PARABLE	REFERENCE	TYPE	TOPIC	LESSON
Ten Virgins	Mt 25:1-13	Prophetic and judicial	Preparedness for Christ's return	Those who intend to meet Christ at his return must be prepared; his coming is imminent.
Wise and Wicked Servants	Mt 24:45-51; Lk 12:42-48	Prophetic and judicial	Preparedness for Christ's return	True followers of Jesus will watch and be ready for his return.
Watchful Porter	Mk 13:34-37	Prophetic and judicial	Preparedness for Christ's return	True followers of Jesus will watch and be ready for his return.
Two Sons	Mt 21:28-32	Prophetic and judicial	Judgment on Israel	The "irreligious" Jew who repents will enter the kingdom rather than the unfaithful Jewish leaders.
Tenants	Mt 21:33-46; Mk 12:1-12; Lk 20:9-18	Prophetic and judicial	Judgment on Israel	In the present age God has transferred stewardship of his kingdom from unbelieving Israel to other stewards.
Barren Fig Tree	Lk 13:6-9	Prophetic and judicial	Judgment on Israel	Israel was receiving from God a last chance to repent, after which God would reject it.
Wedding Banquet	Mt 22:1-14	Prophetic and judicial	Judgment	All are invited into God's kingdom, but only the repentant will enjoy his blessings.
Unmerciful Servant	Mt 18:23-35	Prophetic and judicial	Judgment within the kingdom	Humans need to imitate the forgiveness of God.

6. Practical Purposes of Prophecy

Practical Purpose	Biblical Reference
Important part of Scripture	2Pe 1:19-21; Rev 1:3; 22:18-19
Proof of the truthfulness of Scripture	Isa 41:21-29; 42:9; 44:7-8, 24-45:7; 46:8-11; 2Pe 3:4-13
Presents a proper view of our age	1Ti 4:1; 2Ti 3:1-5; 1Co 7:31; Eph 5:16; 1Jn 2:18
Provides comfort in sorrow	1Th 4:13-18; 1Pe 1:7-9
Proves God is in control	Da 9:27; Ac 4:25-29; Php 1:6
Produces spiritual stability	2Th 2:2; 1Co 15:58
Promotes evangelism	Ac 3:18-24; Heb 9:26-27
Promises spiritual purity	1Jn 3:3; Tit 2:12-13; 1Th 3:13; 5:23; Jas 5:7-9; Php 4:5; 1Pe 1:3-7; 2Pe 3:11-12
Procures moral and social responsibility	Ro 13:11-14; 1Th 5:6-11
Produces an informed student of Scripture	2Ti 2:15; 1Pe 1:10-12; 2Pe 3:16
Provokes a sincere love for Christ	2Ti 4:8; 1Pe 1:8

7. The Concept of Kingdom in the Bible

Universal Kingdom	Our sovereign and transcendent God reigns always. "His kingdom rules over all!" (Pss 103:19; 97:1; 99:1).
Mediatorial Kingdom	Outcroppings of the control of God are seen in the history of Israel, and promises are made of an earthly kingdom "that will never be destroyed" (Da 7:14).
Transitional Kingdom	The kingdom of our age is not linked to any nationalistic identity. The equation of the kingdom with the church, after the fashion of the Augustinian error, fails to see God's kingdom rule as operative in the church but not coextensive with the church (Mt 25:31-46).
Eschatological Kingdom	The rule of God is set up on earth when Christ returns in power and glory, a further transitional phase in which the glory of God is expressed in the time-space order. All the promises of the theocratic kingdom will be fulfilled to Israel (Rev 20:1-3).
Eternal Kingdom	The everlasting kingdom cannot commence until the "last enemy"–death–is destroyed. "Then the end will come, when he hands over the kingdom to God the Father after he has destroyed all dominion, authority, and power. For he must reign until he has put all his enemies under his feet" (1Co 15:24-26).

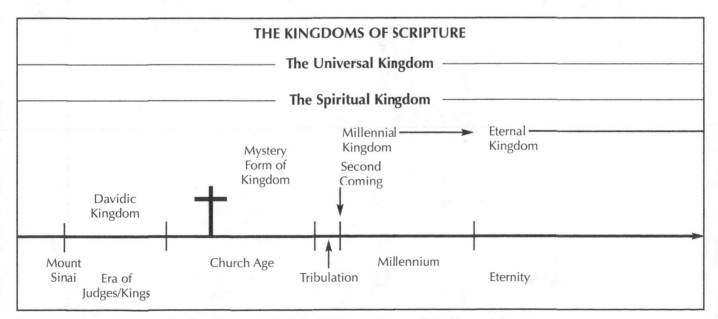

Diagram from Thomas Ice, *Bible Prophecy Charts* (Arlington, TX: The Pre-Trib Research Center, n.d.). Used by permission.

8. The Ministry of the Holy Spirit in the Old and New Testaments

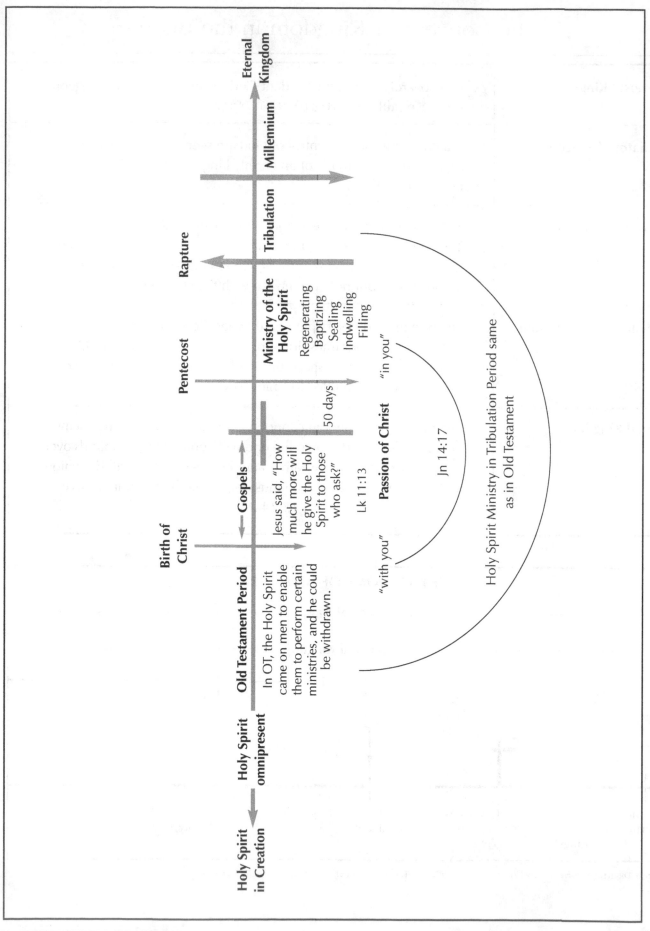

9. Views on the New Covenant

How can the OT and NT data on the new covenant be reconciled? Jer 31 declares that the new covenant is for Israel and Judah, but the NT (Lk 22:20; 1Co 11:25; 2Co 3:6; Heb 8:8; 9:15) applies it to the church. Is there actually no new covenant? Is it only for Israel, or only for the church? Are there two new covenants? Or does the church participate in some aspects of the new covenant while awaiting its final fulfillment? This study takes the last view, as do most modern premillennialists.

VIEW	EXPLANATION	SCHOOL/SCHOLARS	PROBLEMS
Restated Mosaic	No new covenant	Critical • Couturier • Duhm • Schmidt • Potter	OC/NC distinctions in text ignored 1. OC–conditional; NC–unconditional 2. OC–temporal; NC–eternal 3. OC–external; NC–internal 4. OC–no enablement; NC–enablement 5. NC–peace, prosperity, sanctuary, Spirit (parallel passages)
Church Alone	No Israel participation	Amillennial/ Postmillennial • Allis • Cox • Smick • Boettner	1. Ignores OT data by equating Israel and the church 2. NC introduced/fulfilled to Israel 3. Present need to know Yahweh (need for Great Commission) 4. A.D. 70 Jerusalem vs. Jer 31:40
Israel Alone	No church participation	Misc./Classical Dispensational • Darby • Thompson • von Rad	1. Ignores NT data • Christ's Last Supper words • Paul's statements • Hebrews' application to the church 2. Ignores present work of Spirit
Two New Covenants	NC for Israel NC for the church	Early 1900s Dispensational • Chafer • Walvoord (old school) • Ryrie (old school)	1. Same terminology for OT and NT NCs 2. Israel/church distinction too sharp 3. Basis of forgiveness the same 4. Church doesn't possess Israel's promises
Church Participation	Primarily for Israel Secondarily for the church	Misc./Present Dispensational • Keil • Lemke • Bright • Scofield • Walvoord (DTS)* • Ryrie (DTS) • Archer (TEDS) • Kaiser (TEDS) • Feinberg (Talbot) • Thiessen (Talbot)	Support: 1. Primary fulfillment future (Ro 11) 2. Deals with both OT and NT data 3. Forgiveness/Spirit–blessings now 4. NC has new law 5. Rebuttals to above views

Adapted from Rick Griffith, *Eschatology: The Study of Future Events* (notes for Singapore Bible College, 7th ed., 1999), 119a. Used by permission.
*References are to seminaries where these authors taught at the time of position being stated.

10. Contrasts between the Abrahamic and Mosaic Covenants

Distinguishing these covenants provides a foundation for interpreting the OT and NT, especially for interpreting the prophets who look back on and refer to the Abrahamic covenants (e.g., Eze 36-37; OTS, 508) and Mosaic convenants (e.g., La 1:3; OTS, 496). Knowing the conditional and temporal nature of the law prevents misapplying obsolete commands to the church today (e.g., Sabbath, charging interest to believers, tithing). Also, God's faithfulness to sinners is clear because of the example of Abraham.

	ABRAHAMIC COVENANT	MOSAIC COVENANT
Recipient, Date, and Place	Abraham as mediator for all nations 2060 B.C., Ur of the Chaldeans	Moses as mediator for Israel 1445 B.C., Mount Sinai
Scripture	Ge 12:1-3 (but formalized into a covenant in Ge 15)	Ex 20-31 is the heart of the covenant
Between God and:	A person (for a future nation)	A nation
Scope	Universal ("through your offspring all nations on earth will be blessed")	Only Israel received the Law (Dt 4:8; Ps 147:20)
Character and Significance	Grace (promises) Primary (what God will do)	Works (laws) Secondary (how God will do it)
Promises	Land, seed, and blessing (time of fulfillment unstated)	Blessing for obedience and cursing for disobedience (Lev 26; Dt 28)
Conditions	Unconditional: "I will ..."	Conditional: "If you will ... then I will ..."
Participation	Abraham asleep (Ge 15:17)	Israel agreed to obey (Ex 19:8)
Analogy	Father to son (royal grant)	Suzerain (superior king) to vassal (servant nation)
Purpose	Clarified Israel's blessings in general terms to motivate the nation toward righteousness by faith in God's provision of a wonderful future (Ge 12:1; 15:1, 6)	Clarified how Israel could be blessed in the Abrahamic covenant as soon and as fully as possible; didn't restate or expand the Abrahamic covenant, but revealed sin (Ro 5:20; Gal 3:19, 24)
Form	Oral (no written stipulations)	Written on tablets of stone and in Pentateuch
Emphasis	Blessing over discipline/judgment (five "blessings" in Ge 12:1-3)	Judgment/discipline over blessing (contrast Dt 28:1-14 with Dt 28:15-68)
Christology	Ultimate seed (Ge 12:3)	Typified in tabernacle (Heb 8-10)
Sign	Circumcision (Ge 17:11)	Sabbath (Ex 31:13, 17)
End	Never terminated (deemed an eternal covenant in Ge 17:8)	Ended at Christ's death (Ro 7:6; 10:4; 2Co 3:7-11; Gal 5:1; Heb 7:11-12)

Adapted from Griffith, *Eschatology*, 25a, which in turn is partly based on Thomas L. Constable, "A Theology of Joshua, Judges, and Ruth," in *A Theology of the Old Testament*, ed. Roy B. Zuck (Chicago: Moody Press, 1991), 100-101. Used by permission.

11. Signs of the Covenants

God has made several covenants with man throughout the ages. With several of them he has attached a sign or memorial on an ongoing basis. These function as reminders of his and/or our responsibilities to keep these covenants.

COVENANT	DEFINITION	PROMISE	FULFILLMENT	SIGN
Noahic	Unconditional promise not to flood the earth again	Ge 9:12-17	No more sea (Rev 21:1)	Rainbow (Ge 9:12-17)
Abrahamic	Promise to provide Israel a land, rule, and spiritual blessing	Ge 12:1-3; 15:13-18	Continues at present (Gal 3:17), but Israel still has a future in the new covenant (see Ro 11:25-27)	Circumcision (Ge 17:11)
Mosaic	Conditional stipulations for blessing on Israel	Ex 19-31; Dt 28	Death of Christ (Ro 7:4-6)	Sabbath (Ex 31:13)
Palestinian	Promise of *physical* land from the Wadi of Egypt to the Euphrates River	Dt 30:1-10	Land blessed (Am 9:13-15) No sign (that I know of)	
Davidic	Promise of eternal, *political* rule of a descendant of David	2Sa 7:12-17	Rule renewed (Am 9:11-12)	Christ seated at the Father's right hand (Ac 2:34-36)
New	Promise of *spiritual* indwelling of the Spirit (law written on hearts), forgiveness, and total evangelization of Israel	Jer 31:31-34	Paul and the apostles (2Co 3-4) All Israel saved (Ro 11:26-27)	Cup of the Lord's Supper (Lk 21:20; 1Co 11:25)

Adapted from Griffith, *Eschatology*, 25c. Used by permission.

12. Amillennial View of God's Eternal Kingdom Purpose

"Thy kingdom come. Thy will be done in earth, as it is in heaven" (Mt 6:10)

Chronologically Irrupted into History with Respect to Covenantal Administration

The Beginning of History
THE ORIGINAL CREATION
of
the heaven and the earth
and the First Adam,
the son of God

The Renewal of History
THE RECREATION
of
the earth and the
recommissioning of man
through Noah

The Middle of History
THE INCARNATION
of
the Last Adam,
the Son of God

The End of History
THE CREATION
of
the new heaven and
the new earth, where
righteousness dwells

—Eternity Future—

The Era of Old Creation
(Type and Promise)

THE WORLD THAT WAS
2Pe 3:6

Prologue to Covenant History

The Era of New Creation
(Antitype and Fulfillment)

THE WORLD THAT NOW IS
2Pe 3:7

Old Covenant History | New Covenant History

THE WORLD TO COME
2Pe 3:13

Pentecost
A.D. 70

—Eternity Past—
Before History   After History

TIME →
TIME ←

Return of Christ

Fall — Flood — Cross — Return of Christ

Blessing Cursing Blessing Fall Blessing
SALVATION

Cursing Blessing
SALVATION

Cross Blessing
Cursing

Cursing Blessing

SALVATION

Ge 2:16f

(Seed) (Form)
Covenant
of
Creation
(Obedience)

Moral Law
Ge 3:15
Covenant
of
Promise
(Faith)

Ge 3:15
Promise of Christ

Noahic
Covenant

Moral Law
Ge 15:17

Abrahamic
Covenant
Covenants of Promise – Eph 2:12
Ge 6:18; 9:9, 11, 17

The Exodus

Moses

Moral Law
2Sa 7:13
23:5

Davidic
Covenant

New Exodus

**OLD
COVENANT**
(Types of Christ)
Ex 24:8; Dt 5:2f
Law of Moses
Physical and Temporal
(Lev 18:5; Ro 5:20
Gal 3:19)

Mount Sinai
OLD COVENANT
(Instituted)

(OC Fulfilled and Terminated)
National Israel

Earthly Mount Zion
NEW COVENANT
(Inaugurated)

Spiritual Israel

**NEW
COVENANT**
Christ, the New Moses
Fulfillment of CHRIST
(Mt 5:17-20)
(Ro 3:21f; 10:4)
Gal 2:16; 3:16, 22
(Php 3:9)
(Heb 8:7-13)
Law of Christ
Spiritual and Eternal
(Ro 8:1-3; Gal 6:2, 15-16)

(Absolute and Eternal)
**NEW
COVENANT**

(Mt 22:36-40)
(Ro 2:14-16)

CONSUMMATION (Ro 11:33-36)
by Christ
(1Co 15:23b-28)

Heavenly Mount Zion
NEW COVENANT
(Consummated)

13. Stages of the Kingdom of God

	PAST	PRESENT	FUTURE
Time Period	John saw the kingdom as past in the sense it always existed.	Jesus' ministry to Tribulation	Second Advent/Millennium to eternity
Ruler	God the Father (Adam as vice-regent gave his authority to Satan)	God the Father (some say Jesus in heaven)	Christ on earth (1000 years; cf. Ps 2) then in heaven
Mediators	Moses, Davidic kings, priests, Israel (Ex 19:6)	Christ (1Jn 2:1)	Israel (Zec 8:20-23)
Participants	Israel (with proselyte Gentiles such as Rahab, Ruth, etc.)	Church (Gal 3:26–saved Jews are now part of the church)	Entire earth, including Israel and the church (Heb 12:28; 2Pe 1:11)
Type	Political and spiritual	Spiritual "mystery phase" (Mt 13)	Political and spiritual
Realm	Earth	Earth (some say heaven as well)	Earth (1000 years) to new heavens and new earth (eternity)
Entrance Requirement	Faith in God (Ge 15:6, Ro 4:4, 9), shown in identification with Israel	Faith in Christ (Jn 3:16)	Glorified saints: members of the universal church. Mortals from Tribulation: faith in Christ (Rev 7:1-17)
Emphasis	Law (Ex 19-40)	Grace (Eph 3:2-13)	Both law and grace • Law with Christ ruling with rod of iron (Ps 2:9) • Grace with entrance based on faith
Governments	Innocence (Eden, pre-Fall) Noah, the Patriarchs, Abraham, Isaac, Jacob (post-Fall) Theocracy (Moses to Samuel) Monarchy (Saul to Zedekiah) Foreign rule (Intertestamental era)	No government now rules with divine authority over any other, though believers are commanded to be subject to whichever government is over them (Ro 13)	Monarchy (Christ ruling as King)
Covenants	Abrahamic (Ge 12:1-3) and Mosaic (Ex 19)	New (2Co 3-4) Mosaic abolished (Ro 7)	Davidic (Am 9:11-15) and Palestinian (Dt 30:1-10)

Adapted from Griffith, *Eschatology*, 119a. Used by permission.

PART 1: AN INTRODUCTION TO PROPHECY

PART 2

Hermeneutics and Prophecy

14. Biblical Types

Subject	Meaning	Scripture Reference
Adam's status	Christ's achieving of Adam's lost dominion, at his ascension	Ge 1
Tree of life	Perfected life in the New Jerusalem	Ge 2
Adam's fall	The contrasting act of representative justification by Christ, the "last Adam"	Ge 3
Edenic testament	Christ's suffering to reconcile men to God	Ge 6
Ark of Noah	Baptism, washing away sin and mediating salvation	Ge 7
Noahic testament	Preservation of the redemptive seed	Ge 8
Melchizedek: without father and mother (i.e. no genealogy traceable as with Levite priests), a priest	Christ's non-Levitical descent Christ's Melchizedek-like ministry Christ's superiority to Leviticalism	Ge 14
Circumcision	New life made available in Christ	Ge 17
Passover	Christ's sacrifice as a redemptive substitute	Ex 12
Paschal lamb: without blemish, no bone broken	Christ's sinlessness Christ's body, similarly preserved	Ex 12
Cloud at the Red Sea	Baptism as protection in the believer's new life	Ex 13
Crossing the Red Sea	Baptism as the way to God's inheritance	Ex 14
Manna	Christ's incarnation, bringing men the Bread of Life from heaven	Ex 16
Sabbath	The rest achieved by Christ's ministry	Ex 20, 31
Water from the rock	Eternal life provided by Christ	Ex 17

Adapted from J. Barton Payne, *Encyclopedia of Biblical Prophecy* (New York: Harper & Row, 1973), 193.

Chart 14—*Biblical Types (Cont.)*

Subject	Meaning	Scripture Reference
Altar	Christ's giving his life for men	Ex 27
Sinaitic testament	Salvation through the elect nation of Israel	Dt 29
Feast of Tabernacles	The ingathering of the nations to God	Lev 23
Tabernacle-temple	God's presence with man in Christ's incarnation	Ex 33
Ark of Yahweh	Christ's divine presence achieving testamentary salvation	Jos 6
Mercy seat	An "atoning cover" between God and men	Ex 25
Veil	Christ's bodily incarnation, veiling his deity yet opening up the way to God	Ex 26
Priests	Christ's execution of the ultimate, atoning sacrifice	Ex 29
Priests' garments	Christ's priestly purity	Ex 28
Miter plate	The holiness of Christ	Ex 61
Priests' consecration	Christ's devotion to the work of priestly atonement	Ex 29
Atonement money	Christ's atoning for the soul of each member of Israel	Ex 66
Laver	Christ's washing of men from their sins	Ex 30
Sacrifice	Christ's atoning death	Lev 2
Burnt offering	Christ's life as wholly surrendered to God	Lev 1
Meal offering	Christ's consecrated, righteous fulfilling of the law	Lev 2
Peace offering	The restoration of man's communion with God	Lev 3
Sin offering	Christ's passive bearing of the penalty of men's sins	Lev 4

PART 2: HERMENEUTICS AND PROPHECY

Chart 14—*Biblical Types (Cont.)*

Subject	Meaning	Scripture Reference
Trespass offering	Christ's active redressing of the claims of God	Lev 7
A freed bird (at the cleansing for lepers)	Christ's removal of men's sins	Lev 13
Scapegoat	Christ's carrying of sins back to their satanic author	Lev 16
Day of Atonement	Christ's full atonement for sins, presented to God in heaven	Lev 23
Blood, reverenced	Christ's shed blood	Lev 17
Year of Jubilee	Christ's proclamation of deliverance	Lev 25
Ashes of the red heifer	Christ's cleansing of men's consciences	Nu 27
Brazen serpent	Christ's being lifted up in crucifixion, that all who see may live	Nu 21
Levitical testament	Salvation through priestly atonement	Nu 43
Davidic testament	Inheritance of salvation through the seed of David	2Sa 19
Millennial temple	Unimpaired fellowship with God in the New Jerusalem	Rev 21
Gomer's redemption	Christ's repurchase of men to God at a price of 30 pieces of silver	Hos 3
Gomer's seclusion	Judaism's present lack of redemption	Hos 3
Joshua's crowns	Christ's combined priesthood-kingship	Zec 6
Pre-Calvary baptism	New life to be made available in Christ	Lk 3
Lord's Supper	The messianic marriage feast of the Lamb	Lk 22
Christ's breathing upon the apostles	The apostles receiving the Holy Spirit at Pentecost	Jn 20
The Agape (love feast)	The messianic feast, as similarly foreshadowed by the Lord's Supper	Jude 12

15. A Comparison of Christian Approaches to the Interpretation of Prophecy

Typology*	Illustration	Allegory**
The type and the antitype have a natural correspondence or resemblance.	The illustration and the truth have a natural correspondence or resemblance.	There is no natural correspondence. Instead, a forced or hidden meaning is sought behind the text.
The type has historical reality. (The type/antitype relationship depends on the literal meaning.)	The illustration/truth relationship depends on the historical reality of the illustration.	The Old Testament historical reality is ignored or denied. The literal meaning is unimportant.
The type is a prefiguring or foreshadowing of the antitype. It is predictive; it looks ahead and points to the antitype.	The illustration has no prefiguring. It is not predictive; it is only an example. The truth looks back to the Old Testament example.	The allegory is a conjuring up of hidden ideas, foreign to the Old Testament text. It looks behind, not ahead.
The type is fulfilled (or completed or heightened) by the antitype. The antitype is greater than and superior to the type.	The illustration is not fulfilled (or completed or heightened) by the truth it illustrates.	The allegory does not fulfill the Old Testament texts.
The type is divinely designed by God.	The illustration is divinely designed by God as a picture of a truth.	The allegory is in the interpreter's imagination, not in the design of God.
The type and the antitype are designated as such in the New Testament.	The illustration/truth is not called a type.	The allegory is not designated in Scripture.

*For something in Scripture to be a type, it must meet all six of the criteria presented here.

**The system of allegory practiced by the Alexandrian Jews and the Alexandrian church fathers (Clement and Origen) is not the same as the analogy Paul wrote about in Gal 4:24-27.

Adapted from Roy B. Zuck, *Basic Bible Interpretation* (Colorado Springs: Victor Books, 1991). Used by permission.

PART 2: HERMENEUTICS AND PROPHECY

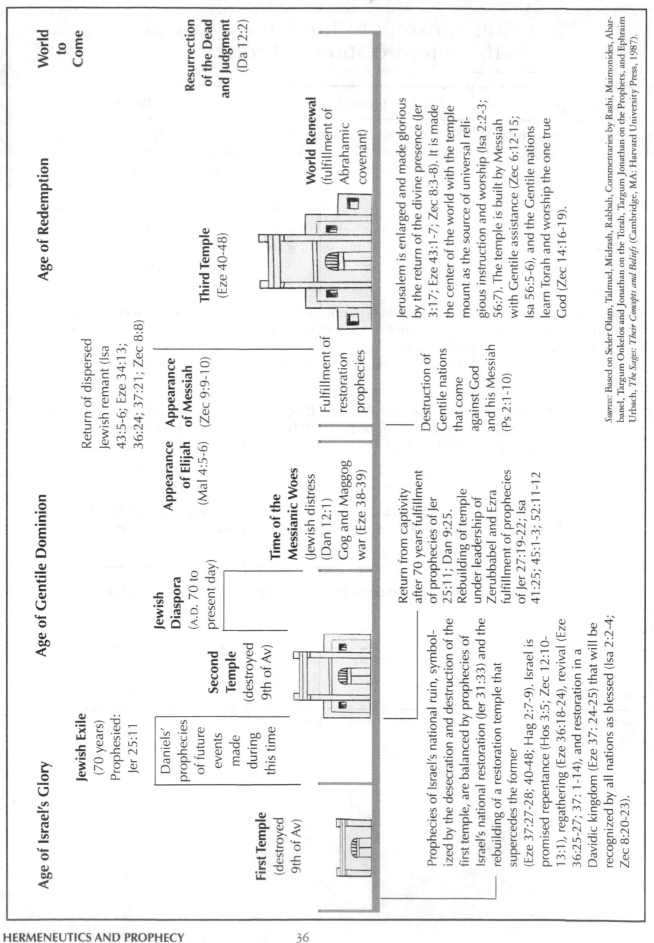

16. Early Jewish Eschatology

Age of Israel's Glory **Age of Gentile Dominion** **Age of Redemption**

World to Come

First Temple (destroyed 9th of Av)

Jewish Exile (70 years) Prophesied: Jer 25:11

Daniels' prophecies of future events made during this time

Second Temple (destroyed 9th of Av)

Jewish Diaspora (A.D. 70 to present day)

Time of the Messianic Woes (Jewish distress (Dan 12:1) Gog and Maggog war (Eze 38-39)

Appearance of Elijah (Mal 4:5-6)

Appearance of Messiah (Zec 9:9-10)

Return of dispersed Jewish remant (Isa 43:5-6; Eze 34:13; 36:24; 37:21; Zec 8:8)

Third Temple (Eze 40-48)

World Renewal (fulfillment of Abrahamic covenant)

Resurrection of the Dead and Judgment (Da 12:2)

Prophecies of Israel's national ruin, symbolized by the desecration and destruction of the first temple, are balanced by prophecies of Israel's national restoration (Jer 31:33) and the rebuilding of a restoration temple that supercedes the former (Eze 37:27-28; 40-48; Hag 2:7-9). Israel is promised repentance (Hos 3:5; Zec 12:10-13:1), regathering (Eze 36:18-24), revival (Eze 36:25-27; 37: 1-14), and restoration in a Davidic kingdom (Eze 37: 24-25) that will be recognized by all nations as blessed (Isa 2:2-4; Zec 8:20-23).

Return from captivity after 70 years fulfillment of prophecies of Jer 25:11; Dan 9:25. Rebuilding of temple under leadership of Zerubbabel and Ezra fulfillment of prophecies of Jer 27:19-22; Isa 41:25; 45:1-3; 52:11-12

Fulfillment of restoration prophecies

Destruction of Gentile nations that come against God and his Messiah (Ps 2:1-10)

Jerusalem is enlarged and made glorious by the return of the divine presence (Jer 3:17; Eze 43:1-7; Zec 8:3-8). It is made the center of the world with the temple mount as the source of universal religious instruction and worship (Isa 2:2-3; 56:7). The temple is built by Messiah with Gentile assistance (Zec 6:12-15; Isa 56:5-6), and the Gentile nations learn Torah and worship the one true God (Zec 14:16-19).

Sources: Based on Seder Olam, Talmud, Midrash, Rabbah, Commentaries by Rashi, Maimonides, Abarbanel, Targum Onkelos and Jonathan on the Torah, Targum Jonathan on the Prophets, and Ephraim Urbach, *The Sages: Their Concepts and Beliefs* (Cambridge, MA: Harvard University Press, 1987).

17. A Summary of Basic Principles for the Interpretation of Prophecy: Seventeen Characteristics

The nature of biblical prediction is:

1.	Historical	Prophecy arises out of real situations.
2.	Transcendent	God's guiding inspiration surpasses human capacities.
3.	Moral	Prediction relates closely to contemporaneous preaching.
4.	Evangelistic	Prophecy motivates men toward commitment to God.
5.	Predictive	Foretelling occupies a major place in prophecy.
6.	Messianic	Prophecy attains its goal in Jesus.

The form is:

7.	Literal	Most prophecy is straightforward in its declaration.
8.	Poetic	Exalted feeling may produce Oriental hyperbole.
9.	Figurative	Context may demonstrate some language as intentionally nonliteral.
10.	Symbolic	A prediction may be acted as well as spoken.
11.	Typical	An event may symbolize to its contemporaries a truth later achieved by Christ.

The fulfillment is:

12.	Necessary	Prophecy is inspired and therefore, when noncontingent, must be fulfilled.
13.	Contingent	Fulfillment may be modified, provided it is near at hand and subject to conditions affectable by its contemporaries.
14.	Analogous	Other Scriptures are determinative for interpretation.
15.	Preferably near	The closest adequate fulfillment is the best.
16.	Simple	The meaning of Scripture is not manifold but one.
17.	Progressive	One context may yet advance through a series of predictions.

Payne, *Encyclopedia of Biblical Prophecy*, XX.

18. Views of the Early Church Fathers on Prophecy

CHURCH FATHER	VIEW
Clement of Rome (ca. 30-95)	"Of a truth, soon and suddenly shall His will be accomplished, as the Scriptures also bear witness, saying, 'Speedily will He come, and will not tarry,' and the Lord shall suddenly come to His temple, even the Holy one, for whom ye look" (*First Letter to the Corinthians,* chap. 23) "Let us then wait for the kingdom of God from hour to hour in love and righteousness, seeing that we know not the day of the appearing of God" (*Second Letter to the Corinthians,* chap. 12).
The Didache (ca. 105)	"And then shall appear the signs of the truth; first, the sign of an outspreading in heaven; then the sign of the sound of the trumpet; and the third, the resurrection of the dead; yet not of all" (16:6-7).
The Shepherd of Hermas (ca. 140-150)	"You have escaped from great tribulation on account of your faith, and because you did not doubt the presence of such a beast. Go, therefore, and tell the elect of the Lord His mighty deeds, and say to them that this beast is a type of the great tribulation that is coming" (*Visions* 1. 4. 2).
Barnabas	Barnabas believed that after 6,000 years of history, Christ would return to destroy the Antichrist and to set up his kingdom on the earth for the seventh "day" of 1,000 years (*Epistle of Barnabas,* chap. 15).
Polycarp (70-155)	"If we please Him in this present age, we shall receive also the age to come, according as He promised to us that He will raise us from the dead, and that if we live worthily of Him, 'we shall also reign with Him.'"
Ignatius (ca. 35-107)	Ignatius refers in his writings to the last times and emphasizes an attitude of expectancy for Christ's return.
Papias (80-163)	Papias wrote that after the resurrection of the dead the Millennium will come, "when the personal reign of Christ will be established on the earth" (fragment VI, quoted by Irenaeus and Eusebius).
Justin Martyr (ca. 100-164)	"But I and whoever are on all points right-minded Christians know that there will be resurrection of the dead and a thousand years in Jerusalem, which will then be built, adorned, and enlarged as the prophets Ezekiel and Isaiah and the others declare.... And John, one of the Apostles ... predicted by a revelation that was made to him that those who believed in our Christ would spend a thousand years in Jerusalem, and thereafter the general ... the eternal resurrection and judgment of all men would likewise take place" (*Dialogue with Trypho,* chaps. 80-81).

Chart 18—*Views of the Early Church Fathers on Prophecy (Cont.)*

Irenaeus	"But when this Antichrist shall have devastated all things in this world, he will reign for three years and six months, and sit in the temple at Jerusalem; and then the Lord will come from heaven in the clouds, in the glory of the Father, sending this man and those who followed him into the lake of fire; but bringing in for the righteous the times of the kingdom, that is, the rest, the hallowed seventh day; and restoring to Abraham the promised inheritance, in which kingdom the Lord declared, that many coming from the east and from the west would sit down with Abraham, Isaac, and Jacob.... The predicted blessing, therefore, belongs unquestionably to the times of the kingdom, when the righteous shall bear rule upon their rising from the dead" (*Against Heresies,* 5, 30-33).
Tertullian	Tertullian referred to Christ in his second advent as the stone of Da 2 that would smash the Gentile kingdoms and establish his everlasting reign (*The Resurrection of the Flesh,* chap. 22). "We do confess that a kingdom is promised to us upon the earth ... it will be after the resurrection for a thousand years in the divinely built city of Jerusalem" (*Against Marcion,* 3. 25).
Hippolytus (d. 236)	Hippolytus expounded Da 2, 7-8 as teaching a literal reign of Christ on the earth (*A Treatise on Christ and Antichrist*).
Cyprian (195-258)	"Why with frequently repeated prayers do we entreat and beg that the day of His kingdom may hasten, if our greater desires and stronger wishes are to obey the devil here, rather than to reign with Christ?" (*On Morality,* chap. 18).
Commodianus (third century)	"They shall come also who overcame cruel martyrdom under Antichrist, and they themselves live for the whole time. But from the thousand years God will destroy all those evils" (*Instructions for the Christian Life,* chap. 44).
Nepos (third century)	Nepos wrote *A Compilation of the Allegorists* in defense of premillennialism after Origen had attacked it and had sought to explain it figuratively.
Lactanius (240-330)	"About the same time also the prince of the devils, who is the contriver of all evils, shall be bound with chains, and shall be imprisoned during the thousand years of the heavenly rule in which righteousness shall reign in the world, so that he may contrive no evil against the people of God" (*Epitome of the Divine Institutes,* 7, 24).

"in the age of wrath . . . He remembered them and caused the root He had planted to sprout [again] from Israel and Aaron to take possession of His Land" (CD 1:5-7)

Program of Progessive Succession of Generations or Epochs (Creation to Latter Days), CD; 1QS; 1QH; esp. 4Q181

Former Wicked Age (CD 1:16-20)

390 Years (Based on Eze 4:4-5)
Beginning with Destruction of First Temple

586 - 390 = 196 B.C. (Qumran sect begins)

Age of Wickedness also called:
Age of Israel's Sin (CD20:23)
Age of the Desolation of the Land (CD 5:20)
Age of the Punishment of the Forefathers (CD 7:21)

Latter Wicked Age (CD 5:20-21; 7:14, 21)

ca. 162 B.C. **Rise of Wicked Priest** (= non-Zadokite [High] Priest) (1QpHab 8:16; 9:9; 11:12; 12:8)

Conflict between the Liar/Scoffer (= Wicked Priest) **and Teacher** over millennial expectations of the sect (CD 6:11; 1QpHab 11:4-8)

Possibly assumed own sinfulness resulted in **delays or postponement of expected prophetic fulfillment** (CD 1:8-9) but still **expected 40-year war** between "Sons of Light" (the sect) and "Sons of Darkness" (non-sectarian Jews, esp. followers of Wicked Priest and all Gentiles) (1QM 1-2)

Past Predictive Failures lead sect to cease setting dates, waiting pietistically at first, then adopting a more militant stance

Some members of sect join Jews at Masada and bring scrolls with them

Scrolls and treasure of copper scrolls are hidden

Members of Sect Die at Masada (A.D. 73)

40 Years of Eze 4:6 (divided into two equal periods) (from Teacher's arrival to end of his opponents; CD 8:52-54)

Predestined Ages Ordered Consecutively

20 years *without* Teacher
"Groped like blind men for their way" (CD 1:8)

20 years *with* Teacher
Sect retreats to desert, organizes as community

Loss of Teacher

Righteous (or Legitimate) Teacher arises from their ranks (able to discern prophetic puzzle) (CD 8:10-11)

Application of 70 years of Wrath of Dan 9:3?

Historic Period of Qumran Community (c. 196 B.C. - A.D. 68; cf. CD 6:7-11)

Romans Destroy Qumran Settlement (A.D. 68)

Destruction of Second Temple (A.D. 70)

Destruction of first temple is dividing point of Qumran history (CD 1:8-11)

Sanctuary of Israel that was defiled (4QFlor 107)

Impure

Impure

History of Israel and all mankind traced from Creation (1QS 4:15-17)

Creation

First Temple (960-596 B.C.)

Second Temple (515 B.C. - A.D. 70)

Sons of Zadok
(Elect of Israel = Qumran community) True Representatives of Israel (CD 4:4)

Applied "northern exile to Damascus" (Am 5:27) to exilic condition of desert life at Qumran (CD 7:13-14)

First failed expectation of restoration was with first post-exilic community due to ritual impurity. This led to founding of sect as "holy members of renewed covenant." Sectarian chronology ignored first exilic community and viewed their own history as a continuation of the first temple period. Sect withdrew from second temple because it followed incorrect festival calendar which would prevent the promised redemption.

Ages before Creation of Mankind (4Q180, 181)

Write *Pesharim*, sectarian and apocalyptic documents that interpret sect as "first Judean exiles to return [in holiness] to the land of Israel and as prophesised remnant that would see eschatological war and restoration (CD 1:3-8; 12:2-22; 1QH 17:14).

20. Eschatology of the Dead Sea Scrolls

Two-Stage Eschatology: This Age and the Age to Come

Program of Progressive Succession of Generations or Epochs (Creation to Latter Days), CD; 1QS; 1QH; esp. 4Q180; 4Q181

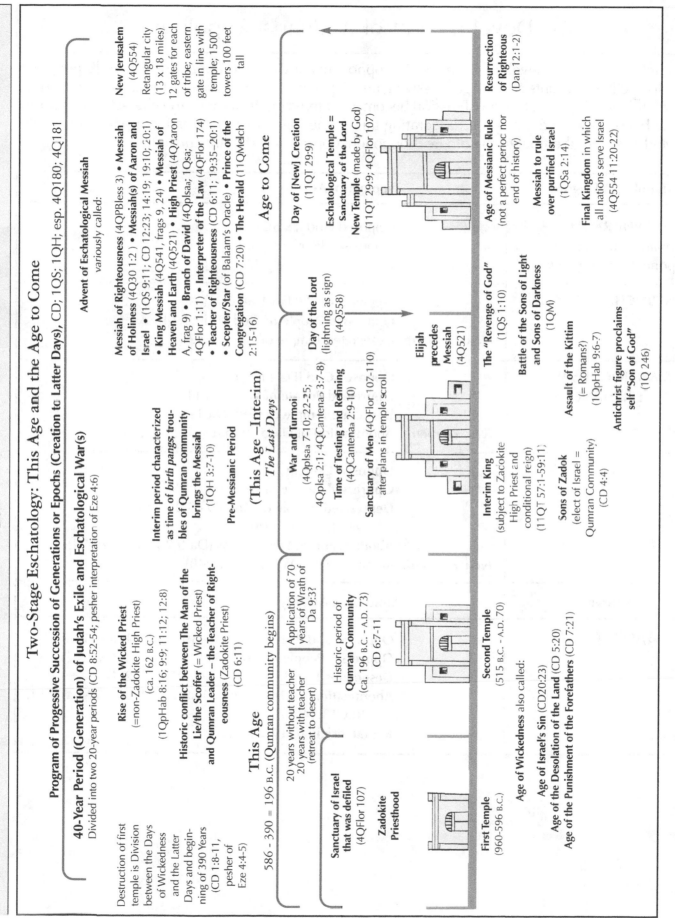

40-Year Period (Generation) of Judah's Exile and Eschatological War(s)
Divided into two 20-year periods (CD 8:52-54; pesher interpretation of Eze 4:6)

Advent of Eschatological Messiah
variously called:

Messiah of Righteousness (4QPBless 3) • Messiah of Holiness (4Q30 1:2) • Messiah(s) of Aaron and Israel • (1QS 9:11; CD 12:23; 14:19; 19:10; 20:1) • King Messiah (4Q541, frags 9, 24) • Messiah of Heaven and Earth (4Q521) • High Priest (4QAaron A, frag 9) • Branch of David (4QpIsaa; 1Qsa; 4QFlor 1:11) • Interpreter of the Law (4QFlor 174) • Teacher of Righteousness (CD 6:11; 19:35–20:1) • Scepter/Star (of Balaam's Oracle) • Prince of the Congregation (CD 7:20) • The Herald (11QMelch 2:15-16)

New Jerusalem
(4Q554)
Retangular city (13 x 18 miles) 12 gates for each of tribe; eastern gate in line with temple; 1500 towers 100 feet tall

Resurrection of Righteous
(Dan 12:1-2)

Age to Come

Day of [New] Creation (11QT 29:9)

Eschatological Temple = Sanctuary of the Lord New Temple (made by God) (11QT 29:9; 4QFlor 107)

Age of Messianic Rule (not a perfect period nor end of history)

Messiah to rule over purified Israel (1QSa 2:14)

Final Kingdom in which all nations serve Israel (4Q554 11:20-22)

Rise of the Wicked Priest
(=non-Zadokite High Priest) (ca. 162 B.C.)
(1QpHab 8:16; 9:9; 11:12; 12:8)

Historic conflict between The Man of the Lie/the Scoffer (= Wicked Priest) **and Qumran Leader – the Teacher of Righteousness** (Zadokite Priest) (CD 6:11)

Interim period characterized as time of birth pangs; troubles of Qumran community brings the Messiah (1QH 3:7-10)

Pre-Messianic Period

(This Age —Interim) The Last Days

War and Turmoil (4QpIsaa 7-10; 22-25; 4QpIsa 2:1; 4QCantenaa 3:7-8)

Time of Testing and Refining (4QCantenaa 2:9-10)

Sanctuary of Men (4QFlor 107-110) after plans in temple scroll

Day of the Lord (lightning as sign) (4Q558)

Elijah precedes Messiah (4Q521)

The "Revenge of God" (1QS 1:10)

Battle of the Sons of Light and Sons of Darkness (1QM)

Assault of the Kittim (= Romans?) (1QpHab 9:6-7)

Antichrist figure proclaims self "Son of God" (1Q 246)

Destruction of first temple is Division between the Days of Wickedness and the Latter Days and beginning of 390 Years (CD 1:8-11, pesher of Eze 4:4-5)

This Age

586 - 390 = 196 B.C. (Qumran community begins)

20 years without teacher 20 years with teacher (retreat to desert)

Application of 70 years of Wrath of Da 9:3?

Historic period of **Qumran Community** (ca. 196 B.C. – A.D. 73) CD 6:7-11

Second Temple (515 B.C. - A.D. 70)

Interim King (subject to Zacokite High Priest and conditional reign) (11QT 57:1-59:11)

Sons of Zadok (elect of Israel = Qumran Community) (CD 4:4)

Sanctuary of Israel that was defiled (4QFlor 107)

Zadokite Priesthood

First Temple (960-596 B.C.)

Age of Wickedness also called:

Age of Israel's Sin (CD20:23)
Age of the Desolation of the Land (CD 5:20)
Age of the Punishment of the Forefathers (CD 7:21)

PART 2: HERMENEUTICS AND PROPHECY

21. Development of Antichrist Typology

Antichrist typology develops from specific opponents of God and oppressors of God's people. It gains distinctive elements as each successive type adapts to the progressive historical situation. Thus, as God's relationship with the Jewish nation becomes centered on the temple, the characteristic oppressive act becomes concentrated on desecrating this divine ideal, thereby creating a paradigm for the expected antitype, the final eschatological opponent/oppressor—*the Antichrist*.

Typological Figure	Typological Activity
PHARAOH (unnamed to emphasize opponent status with God)	Opposed God (Ex 5:2) Oppressed People of God (Ex 1:11, 22)
NEBUCHADNEZZAR	**Opposed God** (Hab 1:6-11) **Oppressed People of God** (2Ki 24:14) *New Element*: Desecrated Temple of God (2Ki 24:13)
ANTIOCHUS IV EPIPHANES	**Opposed God** (Da 11:36) **Oppressed People of God** (Da 11:41) **Desecrate Temple of God** (Da 11:31) *New Element*: Abomination of Desolation (Da 11:31)
TITUS	**Opposed God** (Jn 19:7-16) **Oppressed People of God** (Da 9:26) **Desecrated Temple of God** (Da 9:26; Matt. 24:2/ Mk. 13:2; Lk. 21:6) **Abomination of Desolations** (Da 9:26; Lk 21:20-24) *New Element*: Roman origin (Da 9:26; Jn 11:48)
Antitype	Antitypical Activity
ANTICHRIST	**Opposes God** (Da 8:25; 11:36-39; 2Th 2:4; Rev 13:6) **Oppresses People of God** (Da 9:27; 11:41; Rev 13:7) **Desecrates Temple of God** (Da 9:27; 2Th 2:4) **Abomination of Desolation** (Da 9:27; Mt 24:15/Mk 13:14; Rev 13:14-15) **Roman origin** (Da 7:23; 9:27)

22. Basic Approaches to Eschatology

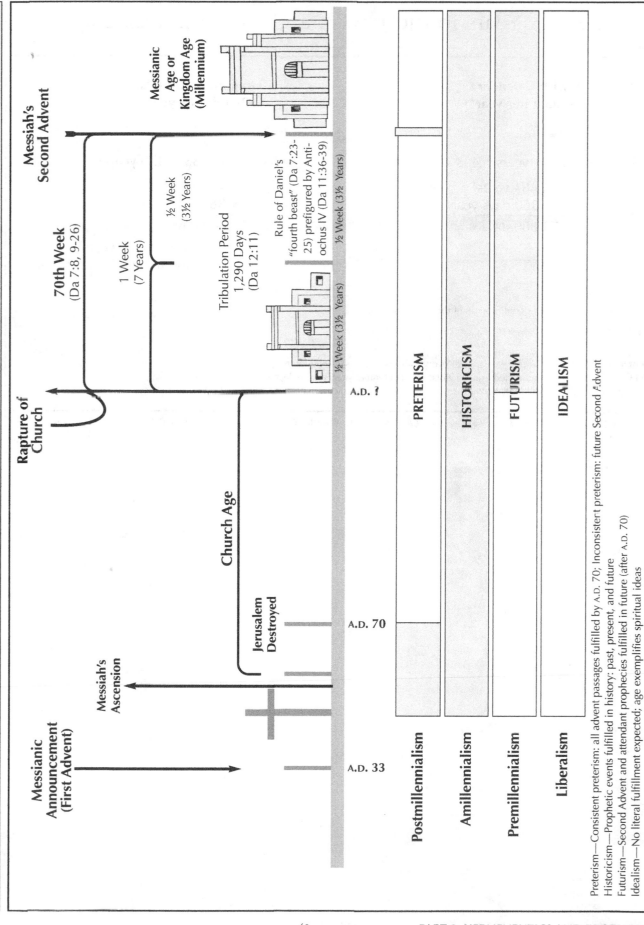

Messianic Announcement (First Advent)

Messiah's Ascension

Church Age

Jerusalem Destroyed

Rapture of Church

Messiah's Second Advent

70th Week (Da 7:8, 9-26)

1 Week (7 Years)

½ Week (3½ Years)

Tribulation Period 1,290 Days (Da 12:11)

Rule of Daniel's "fourth beast" (Da 7:23-25) prefigured by Antiochus IV (Da 11:36-39)

½ Week (3½ Years)

½ Week (3½ Years)

Messianic Age or Kingdom Age (Millennium)

A.D. 33

A.D. 70

A.D. ?

PRETERISM

HISTORICISM

FUTURISM

IDEALISM

Postmillennialism

Amillennialism

Premillennialism

Liberalism

Preterism—Consistent preterism: all advent passages fulfilled by A.D. 70; Inconsistent preterism: future Second Advent
Historicism—Prophetic events fulfilled in history; past, present, and future
Futurism—Second Advent and attendant prophecies fulfilled in future (after A.D. 70)
Idealism—No literal fulfillment expected; age exemplifies spiritual ideas

PART 2: HERMENEUTICS AND PROPHECY

23. The 483 Years in the Jewish and Gregorian Calendars

Jewish Calendar **(360 days per year*)**	**Gregorian Calendar** **(365 days a year)**
$(7 \times 7) + (62 \times 7)$ years = 483 years	444 B.C. to A.D. 33 = 476 years†
483 years <u>x 360 days/year</u> 173,880 days	476 years <u>x 365 days/year</u> 173,740 days + 116 days in leap years‡ + 24 days (March 5–March 30) <u></u> 173,880 days

*See comments on Da 9:27b for confirmation of this 360-day year.

†Since only one year expired between 1 B.C. and A.D. 1, the total is 476, not 477.

‡A total of 476 years divided by four (a leap year every four years) gives 119 additional days. But three days must be subtracted from 119 because centennial years are not leap years, though every 400th year is a leap year.

J. Dwight Pentecost, "Daniel," in *The Bible Knowledge Commentary: Old Testament Edition*, ed. John F. Walvoord and Roy B. Zuck (Wheaton, IL: SP Publications, 1985), 1363. Used by permission.

PART 3

Fulfillment of Prophecy

24. Unfulfilled Prophecy

Understanding the mark of a prophet and the certainty of prophetic fulfillment is a necessary background to a study of unfulfilled prophecy.

THE MARK OF A PROPHET

Dt 18:22 "If what a prophet proclaims in the name of the LORD does not take place or come true, that is a message the LORD has not spoken. That prophet has spoken presumptuously. Do not be afraid of him."

THE CERTAINTY OF PROPHETIC FULFILLMENT

Hab 2:3 "For the revelation awaits an appointed time; it speaks of the end and will not prove false. Though it linger, wait for it; it will certainly come and will not delay."

This is illustrated in the account of the death of the king of Israel:

Prophecy	Fulfillment
1Ki 22:17 "Then Micaiah answered, 'I saw all Israel scattered on the hills like sheep without a shepherd, and the LORD said, "These people have no master. Let each one go home in peace."'"	**1Ki 22:34** "But someone drew his bow at random and hit the king of Israel between the sections of his armor. The king told his chariot driver, 'Wheel around and get me out of the fighting. I've been wounded.'"
1Ki 22:28 "Micaiah declared, 'If you ever return safely, the LORD has not spoken through me.' Then he added, 'Mark my words, all you people!'"	**1Ki 22:35-36** "All day long the battle raged, and the king was propped up in his chariot facing the Arameans. The blood from his wound ran onto the floor of the chariot, and that evening he died. As the sun was setting, a cry spread through the army: 'Every man to his town; everyone to his land!'"

There are a variety of reasons for unfulfilled prophecy. The first is not actually a lack of fulfillment, but a lack of historical record of fulfillment. Following are descriptions of some phrases used to explain unfulfilled prophecy.

LACK OF HISTORICAL RECORD

The lack of a historical record of fulfillment does not disprove the reality or possibility of prophetic fulfillment. In the same way, the absence of a record of the prophecy does not make the recorded fulfillment meaningless. For example, in 2Ki 14:25 we have the recorded fulfillment of a prophecy that we have no other record of. ("He was the one who restored the boundaries of Israel from Lebo Hamath to the Sea of the Arabah, in accordance with the word of the LORD, the God of Israel, spoken through his servant Jonah son of Amittai, the prophet from Gath Hepher.")

FALSE PROPHETS

Mt 7:15 "Watch out for false prophets. They come to you in sheep's clothing, but inwardly they are ferocious wolves."

CONTINGENCY

Jer 18:9-10 "And if at another time I announce that a nation or kingdom is to be built up and planted, and if it does evil in my sight and does not obey me, then I will reconsider the good I had intended to do for it."

Jer 26:12-13 "Then Jeremiah said to all the officials and all the people: 'The LORD sent me to prophesy against this house and this city all the things you have heard. Now reform your ways and your actions and obey the LORD your God. Then the LORD will relent and not bring the disaster he has pronounced against you.'"

Chart 24—Unfulfilled Prophecy (Cont.)

REPENTANCE AND PRAYER

Repentance and prayer is the positive side of contingency. That is, those prophecies that promise bad, not good, are sometimes reversible through repentance or prayer.

Jer 18:7-8 If at any time I announce that a nation or kingdom is to be uprooted, torn down and destroyed, and if that nation I warned repents of its evil, then I will relent and not inflict on it the disaster I had planned.

PRESUMPTIVE SPEECH

Presumptive speech is shown in Scripture where an otherwise inspired man of God is recorded as saying something that does not occur. This is generally accompanied by context that shows he is not speaking for God but from his own mind.

FULFILLMENT YET IN THE FUTURE

Fulfillment yet in the future is the most common reason for unfulfilled prophecy. Two subsets of this category are developmental fulfillment and prophetic telescoping with fulfillment yet in the future. Developmental fulfillment addresses prophecies that have various stages of fulfillment at different times in history.

PROPHETIC TELESCOPING

Prophetic telescoping describes the fact that the prophetic vision is often included in close juxtaposition to prophecies whose fulfillment is widely separated in time from portions of the prophecy.

The list to follow is intended to be a thorough but not exhaustive list of unfulfilled prophecy. In particular, prophecies that are repeated in the same book are treated in their first occurrence. Space will not permit the listing of these prophecies in text form, but the chart below illustrates how they might be rendered with full text.

Prophecy	Reason Unfulfilled
Ge 3:15 "And I will put enmity between you and the woman, and between your offspring and hers; he will crush your head, and you will strike his heel."	**Developmental Fulfillment** 1. In the crucifixion (Jn 12:31-32) 2. In the church (Ro 16:20) 3. Ultimately in the Abyss (Rev 20:3)
Ge 8:22 "As long as the earth endures, seedtime and harvest, cold and heat, summer and winter, day and night will never cease."	**Ongoing and Future Fulfillment** **Rev 20:11** "Then I saw a great white throne and him who was seated on it. Earth and sky fled from his presence, and there was no place for them."
Ge 12:7 "The LORD appeared to Abram and said, 'To your offspring I will give this land.' So he built an altar there to the LORD, who had appeared to him."	**Fulfilled in Joshua's day** **Jos 21:43** "So the LORD gave Israel all the land he had sworn to give their forefathers, and they took possession of it and settled there."
Ge 13:15 "All the land that you see I will give to you and your offspring forever."	**Jos 21:44** "The LORD gave them rest on every side, just as he had sworn to their forefathers. Not one of their enemies withstood them; the LORD handed all their enemies over to them." **And to Be Fulfilled in the Millennium** **Ac 1:6-7** "So when they met together, they asked him, 'Lord, are you at this time going to restore the kingdom to Israel?' He said to them: 'It is not for you to know the times or dates the Father has set by his own authority.'"

PART 3: FULFILLMENT OF PROPHECY

Chart 24—*Unfulfilled Prophecy (Cont.)*

Reason for Lack of Fulfillment

LACK OF HISTORICAL RECORD

Ex 34:23-24 (in particular, regarding coveting of the land.); 1Ki 22:25; Jer 11:23 (compare 2Ki 23:5 and Jer 1:16–the cause of the judgment may have been pagan priestly practices.); Jer 29:21-22; Jer 39:16-18; Jer 45:2, 5; Eze 28:20-23; Am 7:14-17

FALSE PROPHETS

1Ki 22:6 (see 1Ki 22:35); Ne 6:10 (see Ne 6:12-14); Jer 28:1-4 (see Jer 28:12-17); Jer 37:19; Mic 2:6

CONTINGENCY

Lev 26:3-12 (with Lev 26:14-33) Unfulfilled because the people did not keep their end of the covenant. Possibly still to be fulfilled in the millennial kingdom.

Dt 7:12-15; 28:1-14 (with Dt 28:15-68) Unfulfilled because the people did not keep their end of the covenant. Possibly still to be fulfilled in the millennial kingdom.

Dt 26:19 (with Dt 28) Unfulfilled because the people did not keep their end of the covenant. Possibly still to be fulfilled in the millennial kingdom.

1Ki 2:4 Partly unfulfilled because the kings did not keep their end. Fulfilled in Christ.

REPENTANCE AND PRAYER

Ex 32:9-10 (see Ex 32:11-14); 2Ki 20:1 (see 2Ki 20:2, 5; Isa 38:2-5); Jnh 3:4

PRESUMPTIVE SPEECH

1Sa 23:17 Jonathan was not divinely inspired to know that he would be next in line to David. In fact, he was dead before David ascended to the throne (see 1Sa 31:2).

FULFILLMENT YET IN THE FUTURE

Eschatological Future (General References)

Eze 48:15-35; Da 7:9-10 (cf. Rev 20:4); Mt 24:4-14; Mt 24:35 (cf. Rev 20:11)

Return of Christ (General References)

1Ti 6:14-15; 2Ti 1:12; 2Ti 4:8; Tit 2:13; Heb 9:28; Heb 10:36-39; Jas 5:7-9; 1Pe 4:7; 1Pe 5:4; 2Pe 1:19; 1Jn 2:28; 1Jn 3:2

Return of Christ and Attendant Events

Lk 17:26-33 (false security prior to the return of Christ); Lk 21:25 (terrifying natural disasters prior to the return of Christ)

Apostasy prior to Second Coming

Lk 12:35-40; Lk 18:8; Lk 21:27-28; Lk 21:33 (cf. Rev 20:11); Lk 21:34-36; Jn 21:22; Ac 1:11; Ro 5:2; 1Co 11:26; 1Co 15:12-28; 2Co 1:14; Gal 5:5; Eph 1:14; Eph 4:30; Php 5:27; Php 1:6; Php 3:20-21; Php 4:5; Col 1:27-28; Col 3:4; 1Th 1:10; 1Th 2:19; 1Th 3:13; 1Th 4:15-17; 1Th 5:1-4; 1Th 5:23; 2Th 1:5-10; 1Ti 4:1-3 (apostasy in the church)

Rapture of the Church

Da 12:1 (the Rapture and the Great Tribulation); Hos 11:9-11 (possibly the Rapture, cf. 1Th 4:15-17); 1Co 15:49-52 (the Rapture); 2Th 2:3 (apostasy in the church or rapture of the church)

Rise and Demise of the Antichrist

Da 7:8 (rise); Da 7:11 (demise); Da 11:40-45 (rise and demise); Mt 24:15-25 (rise); Mk 13:14-23 (rise); 2Th 2:3-9 (rise of the Antichrist and the return of Christ)

Second Advent of Christ

1Sa 2:10

Second Coming of Christ

Lk 19:11-12 (significant time lapse prior to the return of Christ); Ro 11:12-15 (at Second Coming); Ro 11:25-26 (before Second Coming); Ro 13:11-12 (at Second Coming); 1Co 1:7-8 (at Second Coming); 1Co 3:12-15 (at Second Coming)

Chart 24—*Unfulfilled Prophecy (Cont.)*

Resurrection (General References)

Ac 4:1-2; Ro 8:23 (resurrection of the saints)

First Resurrection

Da 12:2-3 (generally taken to be the first resurrection, cf. Rev 20:6); Da 12:13 (generally taken to be Daniel's participation in the first resurrection); Hab 2:23 (generally taken to be Zerubbabel's participation in the first resurrection); Mt 22:29-30; Mk 12:24-27; 1Co 6:14 (resurrection of the saints); Php 3:11

Believers' Rewards

2Jn 1:8

Tribulation and Attendant Events

Mt 24:28-31 (Tribulation, Rapture, and return of Christ); Mk 13:24-27 (Tribulation, Rapture, and return of Christ); Lk 17:34 (Tribulation)

Millennium

Ex 23:25-26 (the Millennium is seen embedded in the prophecies concerning the initial Israeli occupation of the Promised Land); Dt 30:1-6; Ps 22:27-28; Ps 67:4; Ps 72:1-8; Ps 110:5-6 (Armageddon); Isa 2:2-4; Isa 4:2-5; Isa 24:21-23 (the reference to "many days" is one of two references to a finite duration to the Millennium, the second being in Daniel); Isa 32:1-5; Jer 23:5-8; Jer 31:35-36 (cf. Rev 20:11); Jer 33:17-18; Eze 37:25-28; Eze 38:2-39:22 (see Rev 20:7-9); Eze 47:6-12 (Some see this as millennial prophecy, particularly in light of the reference to "the sanctuary" as the source. Interestingly, there are plans in Israel today to consider constructing a channel from the Mediterranean to the Dead Sea. In any case, it is yet future.); Da 7:12; Am 9:13-15 (millennial prosperity); Ob 1:21 (millennial kingdom); Mic 4:1-4 (millennial kingdom); Mic 4:5 (millennial kingdom, pointing to nonuniversal salvation during that time); Hab 2:14 (millennial kingdom); Zec 6:12-13 (millennial kingdom); Zec 8:1-6; Zec 8:23 (millennial kingdom); Mt 8:11 (millennial kingdom); Mt 19:28 (messianic kingdom); Lk 1:32-33 (messianic kingdom); 1Co 6:2-3 (messianic kingdom); Eph 1:21 (messianic kingdom); Heb 4:9 (messianic kingdom); 1Pe 1:3-5 (messianic kingdom); 1Pe 1:7-11 (messianic kingdom)

Millennial Reign of Christ

Hos 1:10-11; Hos 2:18-20

Millennial Kingdom and Israel's Place in It

Ac 1:6; Ac 3:21 (cf. Ac 1:6)

Armageddon

Ps 2:4-5 (at Armageddon); Zec 12:11

Post-Millennial Wrath of God

Jer 25:15-26 (see Rev 20:7-9)

Judgment

Jn 5:28-29 (general resurrection and judgment of the lost); Jn 12:48 (judgment of the lost); Heb 10:27; 2Pe 2:17;

Final Judgment

2Sa 23:6 (at final judgment); Zec 14:4-21; Mt 3:7; Mt 3:12; Mt 12:41; Mt 13:38-43; Mt 24:26-27; Mt 25:31-46 (cf. Rev 20:10-15); Mk 4:29 (see Mt 13:39); Lk 9:26; Lk 10:12-15 (last judgment); Lk 11:31-32; Ac 10:42; Ac 10:42; Ro 2:2-12; 2Co 5:10; Jude 1:13-15 (final judgment)

Destruction of the Heavens and the Earth

Heb 1:10-12; 2Pe 3:7; 2Pe 3:10

New Jerusalem

Ps 48:8 (see Rev 21:10, 25); Heb 12:22-23

New Heavens and New Earth

Ro 8:21 (see Rev 21:1)

Final Judgment of Fallen Angels

Jude 1:6

Chart 24—*Unfulfilled Prophecy (Cont.)*

PROPHETIC TELESCOPING

Ge 49:10 (The first and second advent of Christ are seen here, the second yet to be fulfilled when "the obedience of the nations is his."); Isa 9:6-7; Isa 11:1-10 (As in Isa 9:6-7, this is a telescoped prophecy bridging both the first and second advents of Christ. The slaying of "the wicked" is taken to be the slaying of the Antichrist [2Th 2:8]); Isa 61:1-2 (Jesus himself interprets this passage in a telescoped sense in inserting a break between the year of the Lord's favor and the day of God's vengeance [Lk 4:18-21]); Da 2:37-44 (The telescoping can be seen to be from one king to another, ending in "a kingdom that will never be destroyed", the New Jeruslaem, Rev 22:5); Joel 2:28-3:1 (Ac 2 records partial fulfillment. But the wonders in the heavens and on the earth point to the Tribulation; the deliverance points to the Rapture, and the restoration of the fortunes of Judah and Jerusalem point to the millennial kingdom.); Mic 2:12-13 (v. 12 predicts the end of the Babylonian captivity, and v. 13 telescopes ahead to the reestablishment of the kingdom of Israel in the Millennium.); Mal 3:1-5 (v. 1 refers to the first advent of Christ and John the Baptist, his herald. The day of his coming is, however, an end-times prophecy concerning the Second Advent.); Mk 13:5-13 (Both the events preceding A. D. 70 and the eschatological future.)

25. The Messianic Psalms

Psalm	Subject	Messianic Verses	NT Proof	OT Clue to Exclusively Messianic Meaning
			Christ Spoken of in the Third Person	
8	Humiliation and glory	3-8	Heb 2:5-10; 1Co 15:27	V. 8, all things are under his feet, which cannot apply to mankind as a whole.
72	Rule	6-17	Rev 2:27	V. 5 is a transition to the future; 7, his reign is forever; 8, his territory universal; and 9-11, all worship him.
89	Line of David	3-4, 26, 28-29, 34-37	Ac 2:30	Vv. 4, 29, 36-37, the seed of David is eternal.
109	Judas cursed	6-19	Ac 1:16-20	Adversaries (plural) in vv. 4-5 shift in v. 6 to one preeminent betrayer. Plural is resumed in v. 20.
132	Line of David	12b	Ac 2:30	V. 12, the seed is eternal.
			Christ Addressed in the Second Person	
45	Throne forever	6-7	Heb 1:8-9	V. 6, he is deity; yet, v. 7, not the Father.
102	Eternity	25-27	Heb 1:10-12	Vv. 1-22 are addressed to Yahweh; v. 24, to El, a change in person. V. 28, Christ is man's hope for continuance.
110	Ascension and priesthood	All 7	Mt 22:43-45; Ac 2:33-35; Heb 1:13; 5:6-10; 6:20; 7-24	V. 1, he is David's Lord; v. 4, an eternal priest.
			Christ Speaks in the First Person	
2	Kissing the Son	All 12	Ac 4:25-28; 13:33; Heb 1:5; 5:5; Rev 2:27	V. 7, the speaker is God's begotten Son; vv. 2 and 12, an anointed one distinct from David; v. 8, possessing more.
16	Incorruption	10	Ac 2:24-31; 13:34-37	Not seeing corruption cannot apply to David.
22	Passion and brotherhood	All 31	Mt 27:35-46; Jn 19:23-25; Heb 2:12	V. 16, his pierced hands and feet, and v. 18, lots cast for his garments; not true of David.
40	Incarnation	6-8	Heb 10:5-10	Praises in vv. 1-5 and 9ff. Are interrupted by a descriptive section. David did not always "delight to do God's will," v. 12; but Christ did, v. 8.
69	Judas cursed	25	Ac 1:16-20	The specific "desolate habitation" lies between generalizations in vv. 24 and 26, narrowed to Judas.

PART 3: FULFILLMENT OF PROPHECY

26. The Jewish Enthronement Motif and Jesus the Messiah

OT Event	Parallel with Jesus the Messiah	Scripture
Choice of Messiah 1Sa 9:16; 16:1; Ps 89:20a	Prophecy in the Old Testament	Isa 7:14; 9:6-7
Anointing of Messiah 1Sa 10:1; 16:1, 13; 2Sa 5:3; 1Ki 1:34, 38-39; 2Ki 9:1-3	Baptism by John	Mt 3:13-17; Ac 2:36 (Christos, the Anointed One); Heb 1:9
Declaration of Sonship 2Sa 7:14; 1Ch 22:10; 28:6; Pss 2:7; 89:26-29	Baptism, resurrection	Mt 3:17; Ro 1:4; Heb 1:5; 5:5
Ascension to the Throne Ps 110:1a	Ascension to the heavenly throne	Ac 2:30ff.; Eph 1:20; Heb 1:3, 13
Reign with Yahweh Pss 2:6; 45:6; 89:3-4	Present reign with the Father	Ac 2:36; Heb 1:13; 1Pe 3:22
Conquering of Enemies Pss 2:8ff.; 89:21ff.; 110:1b-3, 55-7	Second Coming	Ac 2:34-35

27. Messianic Prophecies Fulfilled in Christ

(Presented in the order of their fulfillment)

Scripture Stating Prophecy	Subject of Prophecy	Scripture Stating Fulfillment
Ge 3:15	Born of the seed of a woman	Gal 4:4
Ge 12:2-3	Born of the seed of Abraham	Mt 1:1
Ge 17:19	Born of the seed of Isaac	Mt 1:2
Nu 24:17	Born of the seed of Jacob	Mt 1:2
Ge 49:10	Descended from the tribe of Judah	Lk 3:33
Isa 9:7	Heir to the throne of David	Lk 1:32-33
Da 9:25	Time for Jesus' birth	Lk 2:1-2
Isa 7:14	Born of a virgin	Lk 1:26-27, 30-31
Mic 5:2	Born in Bethlehem	Lk 2:4-7
Jer 31:15	Slaughter of the innocents	Mt 2:16-18
Hos 11:1	Flight to Egypt	Mt 2:14-15
Isa 40:3-5; Mal 3:1	Preceded by a forerunner	Lk 7:24, 27
Ps 2:7	Declared the Son of God	Mt 3:16-17
Isa 9:1-2	Galilean ministry	Mt 4:13-17
Dt 18:15	The prophet to come	Ac 3:20-22
Isa 61:1-2	Came to heal the brokenhearted	Lk 4:18-19
Isa 53:3	Rejected by his own (the Jews)	Jn 1:11
Ps 110:4	A priest after the order of Melchizedek	Heb 5:5-6
Zec 9:9	Triumphal entry	Mk 11:7, 9, 11
Ps 41:9	Betrayed by a friend	Lk 22:47-48
Zec 11:12-13	Sold for thirty pieces of silver	Mt 26:15; 27:5-7
Ps 35:11	Accused by false witness	Mk 14:57-58
Isa 53:7	Silent to accusations	Mk 15:4-5
Isa 53:12	Crucified with transgressors	Mk 15:27-28
Zec 12:10	Hands pierced	Jn 20:27
Ps 22:7-8	Scorned and mocked	Lk 23:35
Ps 69:21	Given vinegar and gall	Mt 27:34
Ps 109:4	Prayer for his enemies	Lk 23:34
Ps 22:18	Soldiers gambled for his coat	Mt 27:35
Ps 34:20	No bones broken	Jn 19:32-33, 36
Zec 12:10	Side pierced	Jn 19:34
Isa 53:9	Buried with the rich	Mt 27:57-60
Pss 16:10; 49:15	Would rise from the dead	Mk 16:6-7
Ps 68:18	Would ascend to God's right hand	Mk 16:19

28. Old Testament Prophecies concerning Christ and Christianity

OT Reference	NT Citation	Subject Matter of Fulfilled Prophecy
Ps 2:7	Ac 13:33; Heb 1:5; 5:5	The divine sonship of Christ
Ps 40:6-8	Heb 10:5-9	The Incarnation
1. Ps 110:1 2. 2Sa 7:12 (Ps 89:3-4)†; Mic 5:2	1. *Mt 22:43-44*; Mk 12:36;* *Lk 20:42-43* 2. Jn 7:42	The Davidic descent of Christ
Isa 7:14 (8:8, 10 LXX)	Mt 1:21-23	The virgin conception of Christ
Mic 5:2 (2Sa 5:2; 1Ch 11:2)	Mt 2:6; Jn 7:42	The birth of Christ in Bethlehem
Hos 11:1	Mt 2:15	The flight to Egypt
Jer 31:15	Mt 2:16-18	The killing of the innocent children by Herod
Unknown	Mt 2:23	The return to Nazareth
Isa 40:3-5	Mt 3:3; Mk 1:3; Lk 3:4-6; Jn 1:23	The ministry of John the Baptist in the wilderness
Mal 3:1; Isa 40:3	Mk 1:2; *Lk 7:27*	John the Baptist as the forerunner of Yahweh
Mal 4:5-6	*Mt 11:14; 17:12; Mk 9:12-13;* Lk 1:17	John the Baptist as the prophesied Elijah
Ps 69:9	Jn 2:17	The cleansing of the temple
Isa 9:1-2	Mt 4:14-16	The ministry of Christ in Capernaum
Dt 18:15-16, 19	Ac 3:22-23; 7:37	The prophetic ministry of Christ
1. Isa 61:1-2 2. Isa 42:1-4	1. *Luke 4:18-21* 2. Mt 12:17-21	Christ's ministry of compassion
Isa 53:4	Mt 8:17	Christ's ministry of healing
Ps 110:4	Heb 5:6; 7:17, 21	The eternal priesthood of Christ
Ps 78:2	Mt 13:35	Christ's use of parables
1. Isa 6:9-10 2. Isa 53:1; 6:9-10	1. *Mt 13:14-15; Mk 4:12; Lk 8:10* 2. Jn 12:37-41	The hardening of many who heard Christ
(Isa 62:11) Zec 9:9	Mt 21:5; Jn 12:14-15	The triumphal entry of Christ on a young donkey
1. Ps 118:22-23 2. Ps 118:22 3. Ps 118:22; Isa 8:14	1. *Mt 21:42; Mk 12:10-11;* Lk 20:17 2. Ac 4:11 3. 1Pe 2:7-8	The rejection of Christ by the Jews

*References that are italicized are statements by Christ.
†Verses in parentheses are not directly related to the topic.

Chart 28—*Old Testament Prophecies (Cont.)*

OT Reference	NT Citation	Subject Matter of Fulfilled Prophecy
Pss 35:19; 69:4	Jn 15:25	The hatred of the Jews (?)
Ps 22:1-18; Isa 53:3ff.	*Mk 9:12;* Lk 18:32; 24:25, 46a	The suffering of Christ
Zec 13:7	*Mt 26:31; Mk 14:27*	The cowardice of the disciples
Pss 41:9 (109:4-5, 7-8?)	Jn 13:18; 17:12	The betrayal by Judas
Zec 11:12-13	Mt 27:5, 9, 10	The end of Judas and the purchase of the potter's field
Zec 13:7	*Mt 26:54-56; Mk 14:48-49*	The arrest of Christ
Isa 53:12	*Lk 22:37*	Christ counted as a transgressor
Unknown	*Lk 18:32*	The sufferings of Christ at the hands of the Gentiles
Ps 2:1-2	Ac 4:25-27	The conspiracy against Christ
Ps 22:18	Jn 19:24	The casting of lots for the clothes of Jesus
Ps 22:15	Jn 19:28	Christ's thirst on the cross
Ps 34:20 (Ex 12:46; Nu 9:12)	Jn 19:36	Christ's bones not broken
Zec 12:10	Jn 19:37	Christ's side pierced
1. Isa 53:7-8 (LXX); 53:8-9 2. Dt 21:23	1. *Lk 18:32;* Ac 8:32-35; 1Co 15:3 2. Gal 3:13	The death of Christ
1. Ps 16:8-11; 2Sa 22:6-7; Pss 18:4-6; 116:3 (last three identical) 2. 2Sa 7:12-13; Ps 132:11 3. Hos 6:2(?)	1. Ac 2:25-28 2. Ac 2:30-31 3. *Lk 18:33;* 24:46; Jn 2:19-22; 1Co 15:4	The resurrection of Christ
Ps 110:1; 2:7; 68:18	Ac 2:34-35; 13:33-35; Eph 4:8	The ascension of Christ
1. Ps 110:1 2. Ps 2:8-9	1. *Mt 22:43-44; Mk 12:36; Lk 20:42-43;* Ac 2:34-35; Heb 1:13 2. *Rev 2:27*	The exaltation of Christ
Pss 109:8; 69:25	Ac 1:20	The replacement of Judas
Joel 2:28-32 (3:1-5 LXX)	Ac 2:17-21	The outpouring of the Holy Spirit at Pentecost
1. Isa 49:6 2. Am 9:11-12 3. Hos 2:23; 1:10 4. Dt 32:43; 2Sa 22:50; Pss 18:49; 117:1; Isa 11:10 5. Ge 12:3; 18:18; 22:18 6. Isa 54:1	1. *Lk 24:47;* Ac 13:47 2. Ac 15:14-18 3. Ro 9:25-26 4. Ro 15:9-12 5. Gal 3:8 6. Gal 4:27	The universal expansion of the Gospel

PART 3: FULFILLMENT OF PROPHECY

Chart 28—*Old Testament Prophecies (Cont.)*

OT Reference	NT Citation	Subject Matter of Fulfilled Prophecy
1. Isa 6:9-10 2. Dt 29:4; Pss 35:8; 69:22-23 (Isa 29:10); Isa 10:22-23 (Hos 1:10)	1. Ac 28:26-27 2. Ro 9:27, 33; 11:8-10	The hardening of the Jews against the Gospel
Ps 44:22	Ro 8:36	The persecution of Christians
1. Ex 29:45; Lev 26:12; Eze 37:27; (Isa 52:11; Jer 32:38; Eze 20:34) 2. Jer 31:31-34 3. Jer 31:33-34	1. 2Co 6:16-18 2. Heb 8:8-12 3. Heb 10:16-17	The blessings of the new covenant
Ps 22:22; Isa 8:17 LXX; 8:18	Heb 2:12-13	Christ's view of believers as his brothers

29. Prophecies Made by Jesus

Prophecy	Scripture Passage
His ascension	Jn 1:50-51; 7:33-34; 8:14-15
Forsaken by his disciples	Mt 26:31
His betrayal	Mt 17:22; 26:21-25; Mk 14:18-21; Lk 9:44; 22:21-22; Jn 6:70-71; 13:18-33
The church	Mt 16:18-19
His death	Mt 26:2; Jn 3:14; 8:28; 10:17-18; 12:20-26, 32
His death and resurrection	Jn 2:19-22
The death of Peter	Jn 13:36
Destruction of Jerusalem	Lk 19:43-44; 23:28-31
The end times	Mt 24:1-42; Jn 3:14; 8:28; 10:17-18; 12:20-26, 32
Future resurrection	Jn 5:28-29
Future rewards	Mt 19:27-30; Mk 10:28-31; Lk 18:28-30
Great White Throne judgment	Mt 7:21-23; 12:41-42; Lk 11:31-32; Lk 12:2-3
Meeting his disciples in Galilee after his resurrection	Mt 26:32; Mk 14:28; 16:7
Pentecost	Jn 7:37-39
Peter's first denial	Lk 22:34; Jn 13:38
Peter's second denial	Mt 26:33-35; Mk 14:29-31
His resurrection	Mt 12:28-40; 16:4, 21; 17:9, 23; 20:17-19; Mk 8:31; 9:9, 31; 10:32-34; Lk 9:22; 11:29-30; 18:31-34
His return	Jn 14:2-3
His second coming	Mt 16:27; 25:29-31; 26:64; Mk 8:38; Lk 9:26; 22:69
The setting aside of Israel	Mt 21:43-44
His sufferings	Mt 17:12; Mk 9:12; Lk 17:25
His transfiguration	Mt 16:28; Lk 9:27

30. Selected New Testament Prophecies and Their Fulfillment in the New Testament Period

Prophecy	Fulfillment
"I will make you fishers of men." (Mt 4:19; Mk 1:17)	Acts; cf. Ministry of Christ; (Mt 28:19-20; Ac 1:8)
"The time will come when the bridegroom will be taken from them; then they will fast." (Mt 9:15; Mk 2:20; Lk 5:35)	Ascension of Christ (Lk 24:50-51; Ac 1:9) Fasting of church (Ac 13:2-3; 14:23)
Suffering from religious leaders (Mt 17:12) Death and resurrection (Mt 16:21; 17:22-23; 20:18-19; Mk 8:31; 9:31; 10:32-34; Lk 9:22, 44; 18:31-33)	Passion accounts (Mt 26:28; Mk 14-16; Lk 22-24; Jn 18-21)
"Some who are standing here will not taste death before they see the kingdom of God come with power." (Mt 16:28; Mk 9:1; Lk 9:27)	?* No specific passage
"Go to the lake and throw out your line." (Mt 17:27)	Assumed
"You will indeed drink from my cup." (Mt 20:23; Mk 10:39)	Martyrdom of James, ca. A.D. 44 (Ac 12:1-2)
"The Son of Man [came] … to give his life as a ransom for many." (Mt 20:28; Mk 10:45)	Crucifixion (Mt 27; Mk 15; Lk 23; Jn 19)
"Go to the village ahead of you, and at once you will find a donkey … with her colt." (Mt 21:2-3; Mk 11:2-3; Lk 19:30-31)	Mt 21:6-7; Mk 11:4-6; Lk 19:32-34
"May you never bear fruit again!" (Mt 21:19; Mk 11:14)	Assumed; cf. Mt 21:19b
"The kingdom of God will be taken away from you." (Mt 21:43-44)	? No specific passage
"Not one stone here will be left on another." (Mt 24:2; Mk 13:2; Lk 21:6)	Destruction of the Temple (A.D. 70)
"One of you will betray me." (Mt 26:21, 23; Mk 14:18, 20; Lk 22:21; Jn 13:21, 26)	Betrayal by Judas (Mt 26:14-16, 47-56; Mk 14:10-11, 43-50; Lk 22:3-6, 47-53; Jn 13:27; 18:3-12)
"After I have risen, I will go ahead of you into Galilee." (Mt 26:32; Mk 14:28)	"He … is going ahead of you." (Mt 28:7, 10, 16; Mk 16:7)
"This very night, before the rooster crows, you will disown me three times." (Mt 26:34; Mk 14:30; Lk 22:34; Jn 13:38)	Peter's denials (Mt 26:69-75; Mk 14:6-72; Lk 22:54-62; Jn 18:15-18, 25-27)

*Question marks relate to prophecies about the kingdom of God whose fulfillment is debated.

Chart 30—*Selected New Testament Prophecies (Cont.)*

Prophecy	Fulfillment
"The demon has left your daughter." (Mk 7:29; cf. Mt 15:28)	Mk 7:30
"She poured perfume on my body beforehand to prepare for my burial." (Mt 26:12; Mk 14:8; Jn 12:7)	Burial (Mt 27:57-61; Mk 15:42-47; Lk 23:50-56; Jn 19:38-42)
"Wherever the gospel is preached … what she has done will also be told." (Mt 26:13; Mk 14:9)	Assumed
"Go into the city, and a man … will meet you." (Mk 14:13-15; Lk 22:10-12)	Passover preparation (Mk 14:16; Lk 22:13)
Zechariah foretells the ministry of John the Baptist. (Lk 1:67-79)	Ministry of John the Baptist (Mt 3; Mk 1; Lk 3; Jn 1)
"Don't be afraid; just believe, and she will be healed." (Lk 8:50)	Restoration to life (Lk 8:55)
"Do not be afraid, little flock, for your Father has been pleased to give you the kingdom." (Lk 12:32)	? No specific passage
"The days will come upon you when your enemies will build … and encircle you." (Lk 19:43)	Roman siege of Jerusalem (A.D. 66-70)
"What is written about me is reaching its fulfillment." (Lk 22:37)	Crucifixion (Mt 27:38; Mk 15:27; Lk 23:32-33; Jn 19:18)
"Today you will be with me in paradise." (Lk 23:43)	Assumed
"Repentance and forgiveness of sins will be preached in his name to all nations." (Lk 24:47)	Cf. Acts (esp. 1:8)
"I am going to send you what my Father has promised." (Lk 24:49)	Descent of the Holy Spirit (Ac 2:1-4)
"Destroy this temple, and I will raise it again in three days." (Jn 2:19)	Resurrection (Mt 28:5-6; Mk 16:6; Lk 24:5-8; Jn 20:6-9)
"So the Son of Man must be lifted up." (Jn 3:14)	Crucifixion (Mt 27; Mk 15; Lk 23; Jn 19)
"I lay down my life for the sheep…. I have authority to lay it down and authority to take it up again." (Jn 10:15-18)	Crucifixion and resurrection (Mt 27-28; Mk 15-16; Lk 23-24; Jn 19-21)
Caiaphas: "It is better for you that one man die for the people." (Jn 11:49-50)	Crucifixion (Mt 27; Mk 15; Lk 23; Jn 19; cf. Jn 11:51-52)
"The Father … will give you another Counselor." (Jn 14:16, 23; 16:7)	Pentecost (Ac 2:1-4)
"I am returning to my Father." (John 20:17)	Ascension (Lk 24:50-51; Ac 1:9)

PART 3: FULFILLMENT OF PROPHECY

Chart 30—*Selected New Testament Prophecies (Cont.)*

Prophecy	Fulfillment
"When you are old … someone else will … lead you where you do not want to go." (Jn 21:18)	Martyrdom of Peter, ca. A.D. 64 (cf. Jn 21:18-19)
Promise of the Spirit (Ac 1:5-8)	Ac 2:1-4
Peter predicts Sapphira's death. (Ac 5:9)	Ac 5:10
Agabus predicts famine. (Ac 11:28)	Assumed (cf. Ac 11:29-30)
Paul's predictions to the Ephesian elders: 　1. "None of you … will ever see me again." (Ac 20:25) 　2. False teachers without and within (Ac 20:29-30)	Assumed Assumed
Agabus foretells Paul's arrest in Jerusalem. (Ac 21:10-11)	Ac 21:33ff.
Paul predicts that all his shipmates will be preserved. (Ac 27:22-25)	Ac 27:44

PART 4

Prophetic Texts

31. Structural Divisions of the Seventieth Week
of Daniel and the Olivet Discourse

First Half of the Week: (Da 9:27a): Synoptic correlation:	**Desecration** The seal judgments (Rev 4:1-6:1) The preliminary signs (Mt 24:4-14; Mk 13:4-13; Lk 21:8-19)
Second Half of the Week: (Da 9:27b1): Synoptic correlation:	**(Pivotal events)** The trumpet judgments (Rev 7:1-13:18) The abomination of desolation (Mt 24:15-28; Mk 13:14-23; Lk 21:20-24)
Final Days/Consummation: (Da 9:27b2): Synoptic correlation:	**Restoration** The bowl judgments (Rev 14:1-19:21) The Parousia and close of end times (Mt 24:29-31; Mk 13:24-27; Lk 21:25-28)

STRUCTURE OF THE OLIVET DISCOURSE ACCORDING TO THE SEVENTIETH WEEK FIRST HALF OF THE SEVENTIETH WEEK (DA 9:27a)
(1) Preliminary signs of the Tribulation (Mt 24:5-14; Mk 13:5-13; Lk 21:8-19)
(2) Midpoint of the Seventieth Week (Da 9:27b) The major sign of the abomination of desolation and the destruction of Jerusalem (Mt 24:15-28; Mk 13:14-23; Lk 21:20-24)
(3) Second Half of the Seventieth Week (Da 9:27c): The eschatological fulfillment with the coming of the Son of Man (Mt 24:29-31; Mk 13:24-27; Lk 21:25-28)

32. Harmony of Daniel 2 and 7

Chapter 2 Nebuchadnezzar's Dream of the Image		History	Chapter 7 Daniel's Vision of the Four Beasts	
Prophecy		*Fulfillment*	*Prophecy*	
Dream 2:31-35	Interpretation 2:36-45	World Empire	Interpretation 7:15-28	Dream 7:1-14
2:32 Head (gold)	2:38 You– Nebuchadnezzar	Babylonian 612-539 B.C.	7:17 King	7:4 Lion with wings of an eagle
2:32 Breasts and arms (silver)	2:39 Inferior kingdom	Medo-Persian 539-331 B.C.	7:17 King	7:5 Bear raised up on one side
2:32 Belly and thighs (bronze)	2:39 Third kingdom	Grecian 331-63 B.C.	7:17 King	7:6 Leopard with four heads and four wings on its back
2:33 Legs (iron) Feet (iron and clay)	2:40 Fourth kingdom	ROME — Ancient Rome 63 B.C.-A.D. 476	7:23 Fourth kingdom	7:7, 19 Fourth beast with iron teeth and claws of bronze
			7:24 Ten kings	7:7-8 Ten horns
		ROME — Revived Roman Empire	7:24 Different king	7:8 Little horn uttering great boasts
2:35 Great mountain	2:44 Kingdom which will never be destroyed	Messianic kingdom	7:27 Everlasting kingdom	7:9 Thrones were set up

Thomas Ice, *Bible Prophecy Charts* (Arlington, TX: The Pre-Trib Research Center, n.d.). Used by permission.

PART 4: PROPHETIC TEXTS

33. Antithetical Comparison of the Little Horn and the Son of Man in Daniel 7

Little Horn	Son of Man
Active figure (vv. 8, 11, 20-21, 24-25)	Passive figure (vv. 13-14)
Dominion is taken from him (v. 26)	Dominion is given to him (v. 14)
Royal figure of the fourth kingdom (vv. 8, 24-25)	Royal figure of the heavenly kingdom (vv. 13-14)
Comes from the earth (v. 26)	Comes with the clouds (v. 13)
Has a fleeting dominion (v. 26)	Has an everlasting dominion (v. 14)
Negative symbol of man (vv. 4, 8, 13)	Positive symbol of man (vv. 13-14)
Rebels against God (v. 25)	In subjection to God (v. 13)
Speaks, but is put to shame (vv. 11, 20-21, 25-26)	Silent, but is honored (vv. 13-14)
None serve him in the end (v. 26)	All serve him in the end (v. 14)
Anti-God figure (v. 25)	Pro-God figure (vv. 13-14)
Attempts to wear out the saints (v. 25)	Represents the saints (vv. 18, 22, 25, 27)
Alters prescribed worship (v. 25)	Accepts what is given him (vv. 9-14)
Overthrows others as he comes in (v. 8)	Others usher him in (v. 13)
Arises in ignominy (vv. 8-11)	Arrives in splendor (v. 13)
Earthly and shameful (vv. 11, 20-21, 25-26)	Heavenly and glorious (vv. 13-14)
Intimate connection with fourth beast (v. 23)	Intimate connection with the final kingdom (vv. 13-14, 18, 22, 27)
Eyes like a man, but like a horn (v. 8)	Like a man, but more (v. 13)

34. Two Views of Joel 2

1. Locusts are one of the instruments of divine judgment for Israel's sins as predicted in Dt 28:38-39, 42; 1Ki 8:37.	1. The imagery of chap. 2 far exceeds the description of a locust plague. A locust plague would not effect earthquakes, shake the heavens, or darken the sun, moon, and stars.
2. Joel's description agrees in detail with an actual locust plague, which is common to that part of the world.	2. The absence of personal injury is consistent with locust imagery; it should be noted, however, that the assault is said to be upon the city, its inhabitants, and their houses (2:6-9).
3. The description of destruction and restoration fits that of a locust army rather than a human army.	3. It is true that in chap. 1, the locusts are compared to a literal army, but it would not be an abuse of simile for the author to use that calamity as the basis for his imagery of the human army of chap. 2. In Near Eastern literature, armies are often compared to locusts and vice versa.
4. The locusts are described under the figure of horses and horsemen, not vice versa.	4. The invaders are actually called people (2:2, 17), an army (2:11), the nations (2:17), the northern one (2:20).
5. The invaders are called an army in 2:11, but in 2:25 they are identified with the locusts of chap. 1.	5. In 2:17 the nations are depicted as seeking to rule over Judah.
	6. The army in 2:25 could refer to 1:4, and the prophecy in 2:21-27 could have a double fulfillment.
	7. Locusts do not invade Palestine from the north.
	8. It can hardly be said of locusts that they had done great things (v. 20), in contrast to God, who has done great things (21).
	9. The definite article makes "the northern one" unsuitable for anything but an invading human army (Zec 6:8; Jer 1:14-15; 6:1, 22; Eze 38:6, 15; 39:2; Isa 14:31; Zep 2:13).

35. Views on the Relationship of Joel 2:28-32 and Acts 2:14-21

VIEWS	ARGUMENTS FOR	ARGUMENTS AGAINST
Pentecost Fulfillment Joel's prophecy was completely fulfilled on the Day of Pentecost (J. Alexander, F.F. Bruce, Henderson, Lenski, Young).	1. The outpouring of the Holy Spirit was predicted as an event that would occur "before the great and awesome day of the Lord" (Joel 2:31), and Pentecost occurred before that yet-future event. 2. Peter stated "This is what was spoken of through the prophet Joel" (Ac 2:16). 3. "Whoever calls on the name of the Lord will be delivered" (Joel 2:32) was used by Peter on Pentecost and was repeated by Paul in Ro 10:13, thus showing that it is relevant for today. 4. The signs mentioned by Joel occurred at Christ's crucifixion (darkness, earthquake, and shedding of blood). 5. Jews from many nations on the Day of Pentecost were the "all mankind" spoken of.	1. The outpouring of the Holy Spirit will occur "immediately before or preceding (Joel 2:32) the great Day of the Lord and after Israel's repentance. 2. Peter did not use the normal fulfillment promise ("that it might be fulfilled") in Ac 2:16. 3. Peter did not quote the entire verse (Joel 2:32); no remnant escaped to Zion on the Day of Pentecost (Joel 2:32b). 4. None of the signs in Joel 2:30-31 occurred on the Day of Pentecost. The signs at the Crucifixion are not relevant because they preceded the Day of Pentecost by fifty days. 5. The Holy Spirit was not poured out on "all mankind" on the Day of Pentecost. In fact, only the eleven apostles spoke in tongues on the Day of Pentecost (cf. Ac 1:26 and 2:1; cf. Ac 2:7 and 1:11; cf. Ac 1:14-15 and 2:14-15). 6. Numerous people did not prophesy, dream dreams, and see visions on the Day of Pentecost.
Continuous Fulfillment Joel's prophecy was partially fulfilled on the Day of Pentecost, is being fulfilled in the present age, and will be completely fulfilled at the Second Advent. (Blanc, Freeman, Torrey).	1. Peter interpreted Joel's words "after this" to mean "in the last days." 2. The Holy Spirit is being poured out today on all mankind by his convicting, regenerating, and baptizing work. 3. The early rain (Joel 2:23) refers to the initial outpouring of the Holy Spirit on the Day of Pentecost, and the later rain refers to present-day manifestations of the Holy Spirit's power. 4. Tongues, prophesying, dreams, and visions were in evidence in the book of Acts and are evident in the present age. (In fact, Peter adds the words "and they shall prophesy," Ac 2:18.) 5. Peter offered the kingdom to the Jews, urging them to repent. The Holy Spirit was given at Pentecost, a necessity for the kingdom. If they had repented, the Messiah would have returned.	1. The term "the last days" in the New Testament does not necessarily mean the present church age. Instead, it may refer to the days of the Messiah, as it usually does in the Old Testament (e.g., Isa 2:2; Da 2:28; 10:14; Mic 4:1; cf. Hos. 3:5). "In those days" (Joel 2:29; 3:1) obviously has an eschatological meaning. 2. The pouring out of the Holy Spirit in Joel 2 will not occur until other prophecies in Joel 2 have been fulfilled (specifically Israel's national repentance and the removal of the "northern one"). 3. The early and latter rains are spoken of in an agricultural context and therefore refer to literal rain (the early rain in October and the latter rain in March and April). 4. Joel does not refer to speaking in tongues. Though prophesying was done by a few in Acts, it was not widespread ("on all mankind") and was a gift that was to be done away with (1Co 13:8). Dreams and visions were not exercised extensively in Acts and are not needed today.

Chart 35—*Views on the Relationship (Cont.)*

VIEWS	ARGUMENTS FOR	ARGUMENTS AGAINST
		To suggest that prophesying, dreams, and visions are for today is to open up the biblical canon for additional revelation.
		5. According to Joel, the Holy Spirit's out-pouring is to come after national repentance, not before.
Eschatological Fulfillment Joel's prophecy was not fulfilled on the Day of Pentecost. It was used by Peter homiletically and will be fulfilled at the Second Advent. (Gaebelein, Ryrie, Zuck).	1. Peter did not use the normal fulfillment formula ("that it might be fulfilled") in Ac 1:16. 2. Peter said "this is what was spoken of" because the same Holy Spirit was at work in an outpouring. 3. The signs (Joel 2:30-31) were not fulfilled at Pentecost. 4. The work of the Holy Spirit at Pentecost was his baptizing work that ushered in the church; the work of the Holy Spirit in fulfillment of Joel 2 will usher in the Millennium. 5. The Holy Spirit's outpouring in Joel 2 will come after Israel's national repentance. 6. The Holy Spirit will be poured out on "all mankind," i.e., on believing, repentant Jews and on Gentiles ("my bondslaves") who also will believe. 7. Peter quoted from Joel 2, stopping in the middle of the sentence in Joel 2:32, in order to capture the people's attention by quoting a familiar OT passage, to illustrate that the phenomena on the Day of Pentecost were due not to wine drinking but to the work of the same Holy Spirit who will do wonders in the future, and to invite the Jews to receive Christ as their Messiah (cf. Joel 2:32a and Ac 2:21, 38).	1. New Testament writers did not always use the normal fulfillment formula to indicate fulfillment.

Scripture references in this chart are from NASB.

36. Contrasts between Luke 21:20-24 and Zechariah 12-14

Luke 21:20-24	Zechariah 12-14
Past fulfillment: "led captive into all the nations" (v. 24)	Eschatological fulfillment: "in that day" (12:3-4, 6, 8, 11; 13:1-2; 14:1, 4, 6-9)
Day of the desolation of Jerusalem (v. 20)	Day of the deliverance of Jerusalem (12:7-8)
Day of vengeance against Jerusalem (v. 22)	Day of victory for Jerusalem (12:4-6)
Day of wrath against the Jewish nation (v. 23)	Day of wrath against the Gentile nations (12:9; 14:3, 12)
Jerusalem trampled by Gentiles (v. 24)	Jerusalem transformed by God (14:4-10)
Time of Gentile dominion over Jerusalem (v. 24)	Time of Gentile submission in Jerusalem (14:16-19)
Great distress upon the Land (v. 23)	Great deliverance for the Land (13:2)
Nations bring the sword to Jerusalem (v. 24)	Nations bring their wealth to Jerusalem (14:14)
Jerusalem is destroyed (A.D. 70) "*in order that* all things which are written [concerning the Jewish people] may be fulfilled" (in the future) (v. 22).	Jerusalem is rescued *and redeemed* that *all things* written (concerning the Jewish people) may be fulfilled (13:1-9; cf. Ro 11:25-27).
Jerusalem's desolation is given a time limit: "until the times of the Gentiles be fulfilled" (v. 24). This implies that a time of restoration for Jerusalem will then follow.	The attack on Jerusalem is the occasion for the final defeat of Israel's enemies (also cf. Rom 11:25, "fullness of the Gentiles"), thus ending the "times of the Gentiles" (14:2-3, 11).
The Messiah comes in power and glory to be seen by the Jewish people only *after* "these things" (the events of vv. 25-28), which are yet future to the events of vv. 20-24.	The Messiah comes in power and glory *during* the events of the battle (14:4-5).

Scripture references from NASB, italics ours.

37. Interpretations of References to Babylon in Scripture

Symbolic Interpretation	Literal Interpretation
Isaiah's prediction that the literal Babylon of his day would be overthrown was fulfilled by the Medo-Persian destruction in 538 B.C. (Isa 13:19-20; Da 5:30-31). Symbolic imagery (Sodom and Gomorrah) is prophetic imagery of the Medo-Persian conquest.	Babylon was not completely destroyed according to Isaiah's prophecy of "as were Sodom and Gomorrah" (Isa 13:19-20) but simply continued under new rulers (Da 5:31)
Jeremiah's prophecy was fulfilled with Babylon's destruction in 538 B.C. because it designates the Medes (great nations from the north) as its destroyers (Jer 50:3, 9, 41; 51:11)	Jeremiah's prophecies were fulfilled in part by the capture of Babylon by the Medes, but no destruction (as described in Rev 18) occurred at that time.
The city in Rev 17-18 is called "Mystery Babylon" (Rev 17:5, suggesting a symbolic, not literal, city representing some future system of power or evil.	The captive Israelites did not "come out from" Babylon (Rev 18:4) when it was conquered in 538 B.C. Therefore, this must be a reference to a future restored Babylon.
Babylon today is still in ruins, even though a portion has been restored for tourism. The site has no significance to the religion of Islam, nor are they interested in rebuilding a pagan site.	The site of Babylon today is being rebuilt; modern Iraq has become a commercial power (oil), an international menace (nuclear weapons), and its leader has threatened an Armageddon ("mother of all battles").
The early church, Reformers, and Puritans unanimously viewed "Babylon" in Rev 17-18 as a symbol for the Roman Empire (city of Rome) and/or papal Rome as the apostate church of the last days.	Zechariah prophesied the return of wickedness and commerce to the "land of Shinar" (Babylon) *after* its fall in 538 B.C. (Zec 5:5-11). Therefore, a future restoration of the ancient city must be in view.
According to Revelation, Babylon is the city that shed the blood of the saints and witnesses of Jesus, which never occurred in literal Babylon. Furthermore, the detailed description of the city is full of apocalyptic symbolism: immoral and drunken, "sailors" cross sea to get there, burns in "one hour," "on seven hills" (Rev 17:2, 9; 18:17-19).	Rev 17-18 describes the city in such detail that only a future literal city could be in view (cf. Rev 18:12-13).

38. Alternate Determinations of the Seventy Weeks of Daniel

DANIEL'S SEVENTY WEEKS

March 5, 444 B.C.
Nisan 1 of Artaxerxes' 20th Year
Ne 2:1-8

March 30, A.D. 33
Triumphal Entry on Nison 10 A.D. 33
Lk 19:28-40

69 Weeks

69 x 7 x 360 = 173,880 days
March 5, 444 B.C. + 173,880 days = March 30, A.D. 33

Church Age*

70th Week

½ Week

½ Week

Verification

444 B.C. to A.D. 33 = 476 years

476 years x 365.24219879 = 173,855

+ days between March 5 and March 30 = 25 days

173,880

* Messiah cut off after 69 weeks–April 3, A.D. 33

Rationale for 360-Day Years

½ week–Da 9:27

Time, times, ½ time–Da 7:25; 12:7; Rev 12:14

1,260 days–Rev 12:6; 11:3

42 months–Rev 11:2; 13:5

Thus: 42 months = 1,260 days = time, times ½ time - ½ week

Therefore: month = 30 days; year = 360 days

Adapted from Harold W. Hoehner, *Chronological Aspects of the Life of Christ* (Grand Rapids: Zondervan, 1977), 139. Used by permission.

PART 5

Systems of Eschatology

39. Views concerning the Last Things

	AMILLENNIALISM	POSTMILLENNIALISM	HISTORIC PREMILLENNIALISM	DISPENSATIONAL PREMILLENNIALISM
Second Coming of Christ	Single event; no distinction between Rapture and Second Coming; introduces eternal state.	Single event; no distinction between Rapture and Second Coming; Christ returns after Millennium.	Rapture and Second Coming simultaneous; Christ returns to reign on earth.	Second Coming in two phases: Rapture of the church; Second Coming 7 years later.
Resurrection	General resurrection of believers and unbelievers at Second Coming of Christ.	General resurrection of believers and unbelievers at Second Coming of Christ.	Resurrection of believers at beginning of Millennium. Resurrection of unbelievers at end of Millennium.	Distinction of three resurrections: 1. The church at Rapture; 2. Old Testament/ Tribulation saints at Second Coming; 3. Unbelievers at end of Millennium.
Judgments	General judgment of all people.	General judgment of all people.	Judgment at Second Coming, at end of Tribulation.	Distinction of three judgments: 1. Believers' works at Rapture; 2. Jews/Gentiles at end of Tribulation; 3. Unbelievers at end of Millennium.
Tribulation	Tribulation is experienced in this present age.	Tribulation is experienced in this present age.	Posttribulation view: the church goes through the future Tribulation.	Pretribulation view: the church is raptured prior to Tribulation.
Millennium	No literal Millennium on earth after Second Coming. Kingdom present in church age.	Present age blends into Millennium because of progress of Gospel.	Millennium is both present and future. Christ is reigning in heaven. Millennium not necessarily 1,000 years.	At Second Coming Christ inaugurates literal 1,000-year Millennium on earth.
Israel and the Church	The church is the new Israel. No distinction between Israel and the church.	The church is the new Israel. No distinction between Israel and the church.	Some distinction between Israel and the church. Future for Israel, but the church is spiritual Israel.	Complete distinction between Israel and the church. Distinct program for each.
Adherents	L. Berkhof, O. T. Allis, G. C. Berkhouwer	Charles Hodge, B. B. Warfield, W. G. T. Shedd, A. H. Strong	G. E. Ladd, A. Reese, M. J. Erickson	L. S. Chafer, J. D. Pentecost, C. C. Ryrie, J. F. Walvoord

Adapted from Paul Enns, *Moody Handbook of Theology* (Chicago: Moody Press, 1989), 383. Used by permission.

40. Jewish/Early Christian Prophetic Scheme

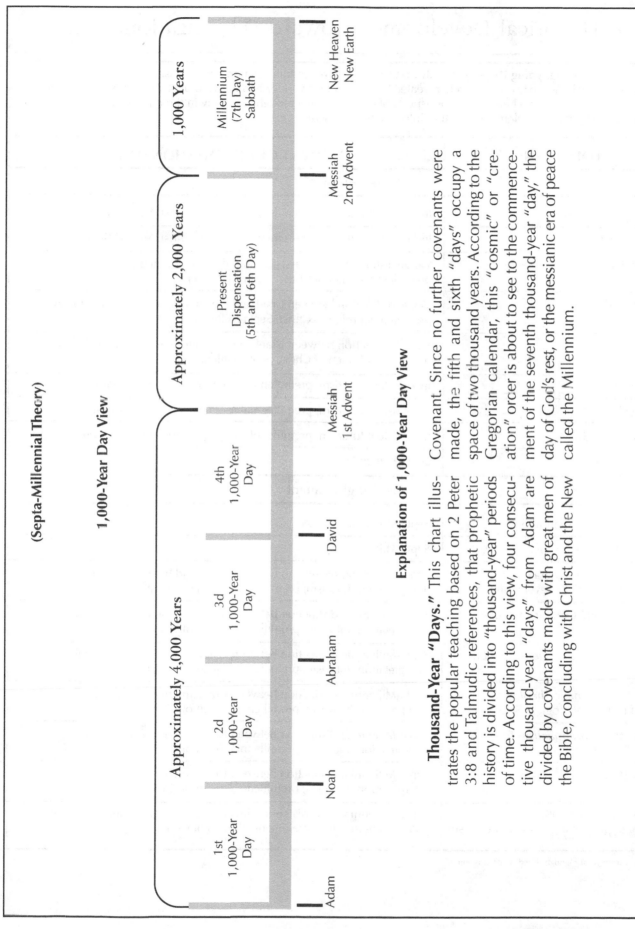

(Septa-Millennial Theory)

1,000-Year Day View

Approximately 4,000 Years				Approximately 2,000 Years	1,000 Years
1st 1,000-Year Day	2d 1,000-Year Day	3d 1,000-Year Day	4th 1,000-Year Day	Present Dispensation (5th and 6th Day)	Millennium (7th Day) Sabbath
Adam	Noah	Abraham	David	Messiah 1st Advent ... Messiah 2nd Advent	New Heaven New Earth

Explanation of 1,000-Year Day View

Thousand-Year "Days." This chart illustrates the popular teaching based on 2 Peter 3:8 and Talmudic references, that prophetic history is divided into "thousand-year" periods of time. According to this view, four consecutive thousand-year "days" from Adam are divided by covenants made with great men of the Bible, concluding with Christ and the New Covenant. Since no further covenants were made, the fifth and sixth "days" occupy a space of two thousand years. According to the Gregorian calendar, this "cosmic" or "creation" order is about to see to the commencement of the seventh thousand-year "day," the day of God's rest, or the messianic era of peace called the Millennium.

PART 5: SYSTEMS OF ESCHATOLOGY

41. Historical Development toward Dispensationalism

Components of Thoroughgoing Dispensationalism: Literal interpretation; distinction between Israel and the church; various periods in which God has progressively revealed himself and his will for humanity; futurist view of history. Theologians throughout history have held to various aspects of dispensational thought, but only in the nineteenth century did some theologians put all the elements together into a system of theology.

THEOLOGIAN	ELEMENT OF DISPENSATIONALISM
Early Centuries	
Clement of Rome (30-100)	Inconsistent futurism; premillennial reign of Christ; Septa-Millennia
Ignatius (30-110)	Inconsistent futurism; premillennial reign of Christ; Septa-Millennia
Polycarp (69-155)	Vague distinction between Israel and the church; inconsistent futurism; premillennial reign of Christ; Septa-Millennia
Papias (70-155)	Vague distinction between Israel and the church; inconsistent futurism; premillennial reign of Christ; Septa-Millennia
Justin Martyr (100-165)	Vague distinction between Israel and the church; inconsistent futurism; premillennial reign of Christ; Septa-Millennia
Irenaeus (130-200)	Inconsistent futurism; premillennial reign of Christ; Septa-Millennia
Tertullian (150-220)	Inconsistent futurism; premillennial reign of Christ; Septa-Millennia
Hippolytus (170-236)	Inconsistent futurism; premillennial reign of Christ; Septa-Millennia
Augustine (354-430)	Septa-Millennia
Post Enlightenment	
Poiret 1687 (seven dispensations)	Septa-Millennia
Watts 1674-1748 (five dispensations)	Septa-Millennia
Darby 1836 (Rapture separate from Tribulation and Daniel's Seventieth Week)	Septa-Millennia; distinction between Israel and the church; literal interpretation, futurism; premillennial reign of Christ
Brookes 1830-1897 (American counterpart to Darby)	Septa-Millennia; distinction between Israel and the church; literal interpretation, futurism; premillennial reign of Christ
Scofield 1909 (*Scofield Reference Bible*)	Septa-Millennia; distinction between Israel and the church; literal interpretation, futurism; premillennial reign of Christ
Chafer 1947 (*Systematic Theology,* founder of Dallas Theological Seminary)	Septa-Millennia; distinction between Israel and the church; literal interpretation, futurism; premillennial reign of Christ
Ryrie 1965 (*Dispensationalism Today* and *Ryrie Study Bible*)	Septa-Millennia; distinction between Israel and the church; literal interpretation, futurism; premillennial reign of Christ
Walvoord 1992	Septa-Millennia; distinction between Israel and the church; literal interpretation, futurism; premillennial reign of Christ
Blaising, Bock, Saucy 1993 (beginning of progressive dispensationalism)	Septa-Millennia; inconsistent distinction between Israel and the church; inconsistent futurism; premillennial reign of Christ

Revision of chart from John Hannah. Used by permission.

42. Representative Schemes of Dispensational Periods

J. N. Darby 1800-1882	J. H. Brookes 1830-1897	James M. Gray 1851-1935	C. I. Scofield 1843-1921
Paradisaical state (to the Flood)	Edenic	Edenic	Innocence
	Antediluvian	Antediluvian	Conscience
Noah	Patriarchal	Patriarchal	Human government
Abraham			Promise
Israel: Under law Under priesthood Under kings	Mosaic	Mosaic	Law
Gentiles	Messianic	Church	Grace
Spirit	Holy Ghost		
Millennial	Millennial	Millennial	Kingdom
		Fullness of times	
		Eternal	

Adapted from Charles C. Ryrie, *Dispensationalism Today* (Chicago: Moody Press, 1965), 84. Used by permission.

43. Dispensational Time Chart of the Last Things

Incarnation	Church Age	The "ἁρπαγησόμεθα" ("catching up")	Interstitial Period	Day of the Lord	Time of Jacob's Trouble (Midtribulation)	The "ἀποκάλυψις" ("revelation")	The Millennium	Eternal State

Incarnation

Church Age

The "ἁρπαγησόμεθα" ("catching up")

Interstitial Period

Day of the Lord

Time of Jacob's Trouble (Midtribulation)

The "ἀποκάλυψις" ("revelation")

The Millennium

Eternal State

Mt 1:18-23; Gal 4:4; Php 2:6-8

Eph 2:3-6

1Th 4:17

Mal 4:5; 1Th 5:4; 2Th 2:2; 2Pe 3:10

Da 9:27

Mt 24:30-31; 1Pe 1:7, 13; Rev 1:1

Rev 20:1-6; Rev 7:26-27

1Co 15:24-28; Rev 21-22

44. God's Plan for the Ages

(The Dispensations)

"A dispensation is a distinguishable economy in God's master plan whereby God tests mankind."

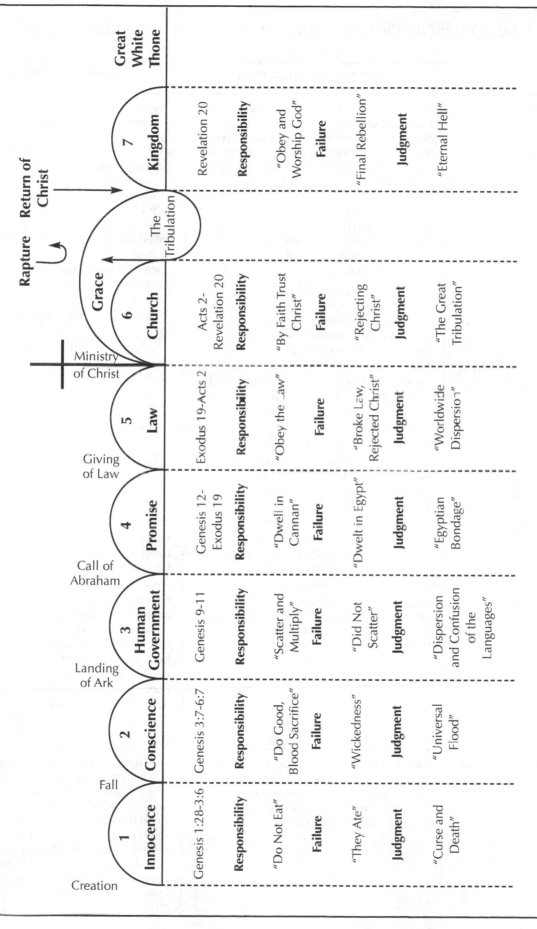

Thomas Ice, *Bible Prophecy Charts* (Arlington, TX: The Pre-Trib Research Center, n.d.). Used by permission.

45. A Comparison of Covenant Theology and Dispensationalism

	COVENANT THEOLOGY	DISPENSATIONALISM
Description	Covenant theology centers on one overall covenant known as the covenant of grace. Some have called it the covenant of redemption. This is defined by many as an eternal covenant among the members of the Godhead including the following elements: (1) the Father chose a people to be his own; (2) the Son was designated, with his agreement, to pay the penalty of their sin; and (3) the Holy Spirit was designated, with his agreement, to apply the work of the Son to this chosen people. This covenant of grace is being worked out in history on earth through subordinate covenants, beginning with the covenant of works and culminating in the new covenant, which fulfills and completes God's work of grace to man on earth. These covenants include the Adamic covenant, Noahic covenant, Abrahamic covenant, Mosaic covenant, Davidic covenant, and new covenant. Covenant theology does not see each covenant as separate and distinct. Instead, each covenant builds on the previous ones, including aspects of the previous covenants and culminating in the new covenant.	Dispensational theology looks on the world and the history of mankind as a household over which God is superintending the outworking of his purpose and will. This outworking of his purpose and will can be seen by noting the various periods or stages of different economies whereby God deals with his work and mankind in particular. These various stages or economies are called dispensations. Their number may include as many as seven: innocence, conscience, human government, promise, law, grace, and kingdom.
God's People	God has one people, represented by the saints of the Old Testament era and the saints of the New Testament era.	God has two peoples–Israel and the church. Israel is an earthly people, and the church is his heavenly people.
God's Plan for His People	God has one people–the church–for whom he has one plan, in all the ages since Adam: to call out this people into one body, in both the Old and New Testament ages.	God has two separate peoples–Israel and the church–and also has two separate plans for these two distinct peoples. He plans an earthly kingdom for Israel. This kingdom has been postponed until Christ's coming in power since Israel rejected it at Christ's first coming. During the church age God is calling out a heavenly people. Dispensationalists disagree over whether the two peoples will remain distinct in the eternal state.
God's Plan of Salvation	God has one plan of salvation for all his people since the time of Adam. The plan is one of grace, being an outworking of the eternal covenant of grace, and comes through faith in Jesus Christ.	God has only one plan of salvation, though this has often been misunderstood because of inexactness in some dispensational writings. Some have wrongly taught or understood that Old Testament believers were saved by works and sacrifices. However, most have believed that salvation has always been by grace through faith, but that the content of faith may vary until the full revelation of God in Christ.

Eternal Destiny for God's People	God has but one place for his people, since he has but one people, one plan for his people, and one plan of salvation. His people will be in his presence for eternity.	There is disagreement among dispensationalists regarding the future states of Israel and the church. Many believe that the church will sit with Christ on his throne in the New Jerusalem during the Millennium as he rules over the nations, while Israel will be the head of the nations on earth.
The Birth of the Church	The church existed prior to the New Testament era, including all the redeemed since Adam. Pentecost was not the beginning of the church but rather the empowering of the New Testament manifestation of God's people.	The church was born on the Day of Pentecost and did not exist in history until that time. The church, the body of Christ, is not found in the Old Testament, and the Old Testament saints are not part of the body of Christ.
The Purpose of Christ's First Coming	Christ came to die for our sins and to establish the New Israel, the New Testament manifestation of the church. This continuation of God's plan placed the church under a new and better covenant, which was a new manifestation of the same covenant of grace. The kingdom that Jesus offered was the present, spiritual, and invisible kingdom. Some covenantalists (especially postmillennialists) also see a physical aspect to the kingdom.	Christ came to establish the messianic kingdom. Some dispensationalists believe that this was to be an earthly kingdom in fulfillment of the Old Testament promises to Israel. If the Jews had accepted Jesus' offer, this earthly kingdom would have been established immediately. Other dispensationalists believe that Christ did establish the messianic kingdom in some form, in which the church participates, but that the earthly kingdom awaits the second coming of Christ to the earth. Christ always intended the cross before the crown.
The Fulfillment of the New Covenant	The promises of the new covenant mentioned in Jer 31:31ff. are fulfilled in the New Testament.	Dispensationalists differ over whether only Israel is to participate in the new covenant, at a later time, or whether both the church and Israel participate jointly. Some dispensationalists believe there is one new covenant with two applications: one for Israel and one for the church. Others believe that there are two new covenants: one for Israel and another for the church.
The Problem of Amillennialism and Postmillennialism versus Premillennialism	Historically, covenant theology has been either amillennial, believing the kingdom to be present and spiritual, or postmillennial, believing the kingdom is being established on the earth with Christ's coming as the culmination. In recent years some covenant theologians have been premillennial, believing that there will be a future manifestation of God's kingdom on earth. However, God's dealings with Israel will be in connection with the church. Postmillennialists believe that the church is bringing in the kingdom now, with Israel ultimately to be made a part of the church.	All dispensationalists are premillennialists, though not necessarily pretribulationalists. Premillennialists of this type believe that God will again turn to the nation of Israel, apart from his work with the church, and that there will be a 1,000-year period of Christ's reign on David's throne in accordance with and in fulfillment of the prophecies of the Old Testament.
The Second Coming of Christ	Christ's coming will be to bring final judgment and the eternal state. Those who are premillennial assert that a millennial period will precede the judgment and eternal state. Postmillennialists believe that the kingdom is being established by the work of God's people on the earth until the time when Christ will bring it to completion at his coming.	Most dispensationalists believe the Rapture will occur first, then a tribulation period followed by a 1,000-year reign of Christ, after which there will be judgment and the eternal state.

This chart represents traditional views and is based chiefly on the study of Richard P. Belcher, *A Comparison of Dispensationalism and Covenant Theology* (Columbia, SC: Richbarry Press, 1986). Used by permission.

PART 5: SYSTEMS OF ESCHATOLOGY

46. The Eschatological Program of Replacement Theology

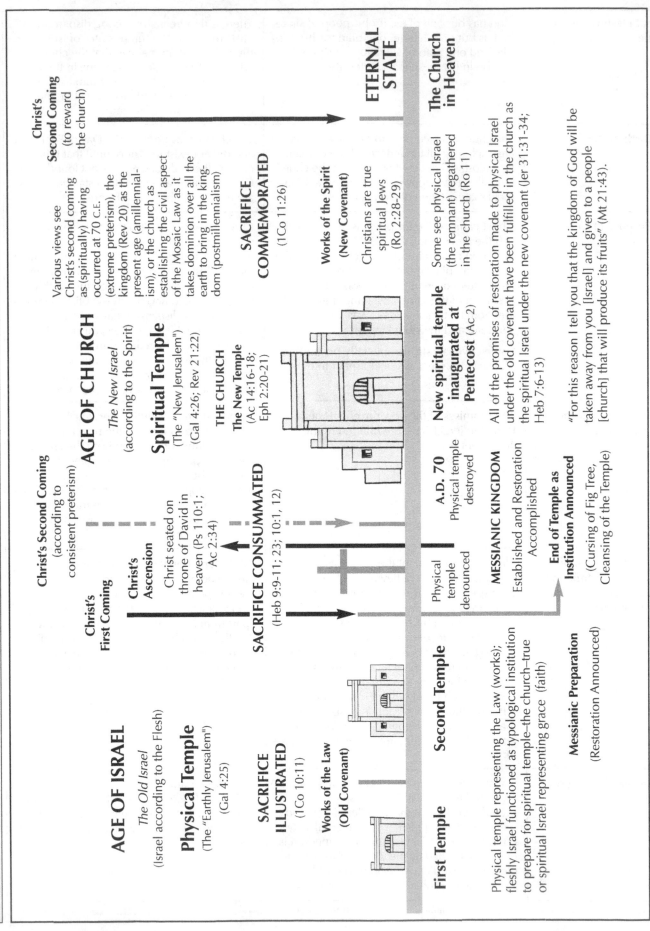

47. Dispensationalism among the Early Church Fathers

COMPARISON OF DISPENSATIONAL SYSTEMS OF FATHERS IN THE ANTE-NICENE AGE

Justin Martyr (ca. 100–165)

	Enoch/Noah (Adam to Abraham)	Abraham (Abraham to Moses)	Moses (Moses to Christ)	Christ (Christ to eternal state?)	Millennium (seventh millenary of years)
Dialogue with Trypho	Chap. 92; cf. chap. 27	Chap. 92; cf. chap. 19	Chap. 92; cf chap. 43	Chaps. 23, 43, 45	Chap. 81; frag. 15

Irenaeus* (ca. 120–202)

	(3.11.8) Four Covenants			(4.9.3)	Millennium (seventh millenary of years)
	Adam to Noah	Noah to Moses	Moses to Christ	Christ to Eternal State	Millennium
Against Heresies	3.11.8; 4.16.2	3.11.8; 4.16.2	3.11.8; 4.16.2-3	3.11.8-9; 4.9.1-3	4.16.1; 5.30.4; 5.33.2

Tertullian (150–225)

	Adam (Adam and Eve; Paradise; Abel)	Noah (Noah and Enoch; patriarchs)	Abraham (Lot; Jews; Melchizedek; patriarchs)	Moses (Jews; the prophets)	Christ ("more faithful worshipers")	"Millennial interspace" prior to "eternal economy"
An Answer to the Jews	Chaps. 2, 4-5	Chaps. 2, 4	Chaps. 2-6	Chaps. 2-6	*Apology* chap. 21	*Apology* chap. 49
Against Praxeas	Chap. 16	Chap. 16	Chap. 16	Chap.16	*Against Marcion* chaps. 3-4, 20	*On the Resurrection of the Flesh* chaps. 59, 61

Victorinus of Pettau (d. ca. 304)

Four Generations of People

	Adam to Noah	Noah to Abraham	Abraham to Moses	Moses to Christ	Millennium (seventh millenary of years)
On the Creation of the World					Millennium (seventh millenary of years)

Methodius (d. 311)

(Jdg 9:8-15) Four Trees/Laws (Disc. 10, chap. 2)

	Adam to Noah (Fig tree)	Noah to Abraham (Vine)	Moses to Christ (Olive tree)	Apostles to Millennium (Bramble)	Millennium (seventh millenary of years) = "new dispensation"
Banquet of the Ten Virgins	Disc. 10 chaps. 2-4; disc. 7 chaps. 4-5, 7	Disc. 10 chaps. 2-4; disc. 7 chaps. 4-7	Disc. 10 chaps. 2-4; disc. 7 chaps. 4-5, 7	Disc. 10 chaps. 2-3; disc. 7 chaps. 4-5, 7	Disc. 4 chap.5; disc. 7 chap. 3; disc. 8 chap. 11; disc.9 chap. 2

*Alternate system for Irenaeus (based on Greek text) is first covenant under Noah; second covenant (Law) under Abraham; third covenant (Law) under Moses; and fourth covenant (Gospel) under Christ. (Alexander Roberts and James Donaldson, eds., *Ante-Nicene Fathers*, Grand Rapids: Wm. B. Eerdmans, 1973): 1:429, n. 3.

Adapted from Larry Crutchfield, "Ages and Dispensations in the Ante-Nicene Fathers," part 2 of "Rudiments of Dispensationalism in the Ante-Nicene Period," *Bibliotheca Sacra* 144, no. 576 (October-December 1987): 400-401.

PART 5: SYSTEMS OF ESCHATOLOGY

48. The Dispensations of Justin Martyr (ca. 100-165)

Chapter references are from Dialogue with Trypho

	I (Chaps. 27, 92) Adam to Abraham	II (Chaps. 19, 92) Abraham to Moses	III (Chaps. 43, 92) Old Covenant: Law (Chap. 67) Moses to Christ	IV (Chaps. 22, 42, 45) New Covenant: Gospel (Chap. 67) Christ to Eternal State?
Representative of Dispensation	Enoch and Noah (chaps. 43, 92)	Abraham (chaps. 23, 43, 92)	Moses (chaps. 23, 67, 92)	Christ (chaps. 23, 43)
Characteristic of Dispensation	Nonobservance of rites, i.e., no circumcision, sabbaths, sacrifices, offerings, or feasts (chaps. 19, 23, 27, 46, 92)	Circumcision (chaps. 23, 43, 46, 92)	Circumcision plus sacrifices, feasts, sabbaths, and offerings (or oblations) (chaps. 23, 43, 92)	All former rites, i.e., circumcision, sacrifices, etc., ended; there is now circumcision of heart and gifts of the Holy Spirit (chaps. 43, 87)
Reason for Change in Dispensation	New institutions were commanded because of sin, hardness of heart, failure (chaps. 16, 23, 43, 92)	Circumcision given as sign for evil done to Christ, prophets, Christians; type of true circumcision (chaps. 16, 41)	Sacrifices/oblations instituted to combat idolatry; sabbaths to be memorial to God (chaps. 19, 21-22, 92)	With advent of Christ, no further need for circumcision, sabbaths, etc.; new covenant promised (chaps. 23, 43)
Means of Salvation in Dispensation	Individual righteousness, i.e., they were circumcised of heart (chaps. 27-28, 43)	Individual righteousness, i.e., Abraham declared righteous/ justified by faith, not circumcision (chaps. 23, 92)	Individual righteousness, i.e., those who lived by the law shall be saved through Christ (chaps. 45, 47)	Individual righteousness, i.e., spiritual circumcision of heart like Enoch, et al.; all may obtain it (chaps. 43, 45)

The means of salvation in every age is individual righteousness, resulting from faith in God and through the death of Christ.

←——————— 7,000 YEARS ———————→

49. Dispensational Features in the Patristic Period

Church Father	Dispensational Features			
	Sex-/Septa-Millennial Tradition	Dispensational Distinctions	Premillennialism	Imminency
Clement of Rome (ca. 90-100)			x?	x
Ignatius of Antioch (d. ca. 98/117)			x?	x
Polycarp (70-155/60)			x?	
Papias (ca. 60-130/155)			x	
The Didache (before end of first century)			x?†	x
The Epistle of Barnabas (ca. 70-100 or 117-138)	x		x	
The Shepherd of Hermas (ca. 96 or ca. 140-150)			x?	x‡
Justin Martyr (ca. 100-165)	x	x	x†	
Melito of Sardis (second century)			x?	
Theophilius of Antioch (115-181)	x			
Apollinaris of Hierapolis (ca. 175)			x?	
Irenaeus (ca. 120-202)	x	x	x†	x‡
Hippolytus (d. ca. 236)	x		x*	x
Clement of Alexandria (ca. 150-220)	x?	x?		
Tertullian (150-225)	x?	x	x?†	x
Julius Africanus (d. ca. 240)	x			
Cyprian (ca. 200-258)	x		x	x
Nepos (ca. 230-250)			x	
Coracion (ca. 230-280)			x*	
Commodianus (ca. 200-ca. 275)	x		x?†	
Victorinus of Pettau (d. ca. 304)	x	x	x	
Methodius (d. 311)	x	x	x	
Lactantius (ca. 240-320)	x		x?†	
Hilary (ca. 300-367)	x			
Apollinaris of Laodicea (ca. 310-ca. 390)			x	
Jerome (ca. 340-420)	x?		amillennial	
Augustine (354-430)	x	x	x*	
Ambrosiaster (366-384)			x	
Theodoret (ca. 390-457)		x?	amillennial	
Cassiodorus (ca. 477-ca. 570)	x?			
Gregory the Great (ca. 546-604)	x?			
Isidore of Seville (d. 636)	x?			
Andrew of Crete (ca. 660-740)	x?			
John of Damascus (ca. 200-ca. 275)	x			

x = View held
? = Position questioned; not based on primary sources
* = View later retracted

† = Belief in double resurrection
‡ = Possible pretribulational reference

Adapted from Larry Crutchfield, "Israel and the Church in the Ante-Nicene Fathers," part 1 of "Rudiments of Dispensationalism in the Ante-Nicene Period," *Bibliotheca Sacra* 144, no. 575 (July-September 1987): 272-73.

PART 5: SYSTEMS OF ESCHATOLOGY

50. Responses to Dispensational Problem Passages

Passages Used to Equate Israel and the Church	Dispensational Responses
The church is the "seed of Abraham" (Gal 3:7; 4:31), which in the OT refers only to Israel. So isn't the church the "new Israel"?	The church is the *spiritual* seed of Abraham, but this doesn't mean it replaces the physical seed so that Israel is done away with permanently (cf. Ro 11:1-2, 11, 15, 25)
"Neither circumcision nor uncircumcision means anything; what counts is a new creation. Peace and mercy to all who follow this rule, even to the Israel of God" (Gal 6:15-16)	Paul doesn't say that all who follow the rule (i.e., Christians) are the "true Israel." He had just attacked the Jewish legalists, so it makes better sense that he announced blessing on Jews who had forsaken legalism to truly follow Christ.
The church is called the "true circumcision" (Php 3:3 NASB)	The comparison is not between the church and Israel but between the church and legalistic Jews
Jesus told Pilate his kingdom "is not of this world" but "from another place" (Jn 18:36)	Christ did not comment on the *place* of his kingdom. He said the *source* of his kingdom was heaven. He did not say that this kingdom could not eventually be established on earth.
"Once, having been asked by the Pharisees when the kingdom of God would come, Jesus replied, 'The kingdom of God does not come with your careful observation, nor will people say, "Here it is," or "There it is," because the kingdom of God is within you'" (Lk 17:20-21). Isn't this amillennialism?	"Within you" cannot refer to a spiritual rather than literal kingdom. Christ spoke this to unbelieving Pharisees who rejected him as Messiah, so the kingdom was not *within them!* A better translation is "the kingdom of God is *in your midst*" (the King stood right before them). "All they needed to do was acknowledge that He is indeed the Messiah who could bring in the kingdom—and then the kingdom would come" (John Martin, "Luke," *Bible Knowledge Commentary,* 2:249.
Am 9:11-12 says that the Davidic Covenant will be fulfilled, and James quoted this prophecy to say that the rebuilt house of David is the church, which was used to preach the gospel to the Gentiles (Ac 15:15-18).	James did not say that Amos was *fulfilled* in the church, only that Gentile inclusion ("the remnant of men") agreed with the OT prophets. Also, the "return" (Ac 15:16) is used of a literal return (cf. Ac 5:22) that precedes the fulfillment of Amos's prophecy. This means Christ's return will precede the reestablishment of David's throne. Christ's present ministry at the Father's right hand (Ro 8:34) is not associated elsewhere in the NT with David's throne; only when Christ returns will he occupy this throne (Mt 19:28; Stanley Toussaint, "Acts," *Bible Knowledge Commentary,* 2:394).
Jer 31:31-34 refers to Israel's new covenant, which the NT applies to the church (Heb 8), thus equating Israel with the church.	Not all of Jeremiah's descriptions are applied (e.g., everyone does not know the Lord), so the church has only a preliminary fulfillment of this prophecy (cf. pp. 23-25).

Adapted from Griffith, *Eschatology,* 132a. Used by permission.

51. Three Stages of Dispensationalism

	CLASSICAL	REVISED	PROGRESSIVE
Other Names	Essentialist (by progressives)	Normative (by Ryrie)	Nondispensational (by some classical/revised)
Dates	1830-1952	1952-present	1987-present
Scholars	Darby, Scofield, Chafer	McClain, Walvoord, Pentecost, Ryrie	Bock, Blaising, Saucy
Dispensations	Seven	Four or more	Three or more
Schools	Dallas (until 1952)	Dallas (1952-present), Talbot, Western, Moody, Grace	Dallas, Talbot
Covenants	Davidic future Two new covenants	Davidic future One new covenant*	Davidic present One new covenant
Continuity	Sharp discontinuity	More continuity	Even greater continuity
Peoples	Two separate programs: Israel–earthly Church–heavenly	Converging programs: earthly/heavenly distinctions minimal	One people: the church continues program with Israel until Israel believes
Believers of Daniel's 70th Week	Tribulation saints who are not part of the church	Tribulation saints who are not part of the church	Tribulation saints who are part of the church
Church Age	Parenthesis in God's program with Israel	Parenthesis in God's program with Israel	Not a parenthesis but a progressive outworking of God's program
Postponement Theory	Belief that the kingdom was postponed due to Israel's rejection	Believed by many but de-emphasized	Not taught due to progressive fulfillment of the kingdom
Kingdom	Totally future	Mostly future (majority) or totally future (some)	Present now, though fullest dimensions are future
Spirit during Tribulation	Absent and not indwelling	Present but not indwelling	Present and indwelling
Sermon on the Mount	Millennial principles	Present ethics while anticipating kingdom	Present ethics while anticipating kingdom?

*Ryrie teaches that there is no new covenant in effect today. In his view, the covenant is not inaugurated now but only paid for: "In other words, clearly our Lord paid for sins that will be forgiven when the new covenant is in force" (*Dispensationalism Today,* 172). This is a minority view among revised dispensationalists, most of whom acknowledge that the church now participates in some aspects of the new covenant.

Adapted from Griffith, *Eschatology*, 132b. Used by permission.

PART 5: SYSTEMS OF ESCHATOLOGY

PART 6

The Rapture and the Second Coming

52. Views on the Rapture

PRETRIBULATION

Statement of View	Christ will come for his saints; afterward he will come with his saints. The first stage of Christ's coming is called the Rapture; the second is called the Revelation. The older school emphasized the issue of imminency. In recent days, however, the crux of the pretribulation position centers more on God's wrath and whether the church is called to experience any or all of it during the Tribulation.
Proponents	John F. Walvoord, J. Dwight Pentecost, John Feinberg, Paul Feinberg, Herman Hoyt, Charles Ryrie, Rene Pache, Henry C. Thiessen, Leon Wood, Hal Lindsey, Alva McClain, John A. Sproul, Richard Mayhue.

Arguments For	Arguments Against
The Bible says that Christians (the church) are exempt from divine wrath (1Th 1:10). This exemption does not mean that the church does not experience trials, persecution, or suffering.	Christians are exempt from God's wrath (ὀργή), but the majority of passages dealing with tribulation (θλῖψις) refer to the tribulation that believers suffer. Exemption from wrath does not mean exemption from tribulation. Also, if Christians are exempt from the wrath of the Tribulation, those who believe during the Tribulation would need to be raptured at conversion.
Believers are also exempt from the time of wrath recorded in Rev 3:10. This is supported by the way the Greek preposition ek (ἐκ) is used in this passage.	Normative meaning of ek (ἐκ) is "out from the midst of" and does not require a snatching from trial. It can mean being kept from tribulation without being taken from trial. The normal preposition for "keeping away from" is ajpo.
All positions of Tribulation Rapture predict a millennial kingdom. The pretribulation position calls for living, non-glorified believers to enter the kingdom, thus to repopulate the kingdom (Zec 12:10-13:1; Ro 11:26).	The 144,000 of Revelation can populate the earth during the time of the Millennium.
A clear distinction is made between the Rapture and the Revelation, an interval of time. This is consistent with various Scriptures that discuss both of these events. The Rapture: Jn 14:1-14; 1Co 15:51-58; 1Th 4:13-18. The Revelation, or the second coming of Christ: Zec 14; Mt 24:29-31; Mk 13:24-27; Lk 21:25-27; Rev 19.	The "blessed hope" and "glorious appearing" are the same events (Rapture and Revelation). The New Testament speaks of one Second Coming, not of two comings or a coming in two stages. The distinction may be in the nature of the events, not in time differences.
Christ's return is imminent. Since Christ may return at any time, believers have an attitude of expectancy (Tit 2:13). There are no preparatory warnings of an impending tribulation for the church-age believers (Ac 20:29-30; 2Pe 2:1; 1Jn 4:1-3).	Imminency for the apostles and the early church revolved around the second coming of Christ. Thus, the Rapture and the Revelation are coterminous, not separate (Mt 24:3, 27, 37, 39; 2Th 2:8; Jas 5:7-8; 1Jn 2:28). Also, 2Th 2:1-10 may list events to be expected before the Rapture.
A literal Tribulation is given in Rev 6-19. There is no mention of the church (argument from silence) in Rev 4-18.	Much language in Rev 6-19 is figurative; the Tribulation may be as well. Argument from silence is inherently weak reasoning.
The Restrainer mentioned in 2Th 2:1-12 is the Holy Spirit indwelling the church. He must remove her (the church) before the Tribulation begins.	The Holy Spirit's indwelling ministry is not equivalent to his restraining work. Also, this passage does not clearly equate the Restrainer with the Holy Spirit, or the removal of the restraint with a rapture of the church.

Several portions of this chart are adapted from Millard J. Erickson, *Christian Theology*, vol. 3 (Grand Rapids: Baker, 1985), 1149-1224. Also from Gleason L. Archer Jr., Paul D. Feinberg, Douglas J. Moo, and Richard R. Reiter, *The Rapture: Pre-, Mid-, Post-Tribulational?* (Grand Rapids: Zondervan, 1984).

Chart 52—*Views on the Rapture (Cont.)*

PARTIAL RAPTURE	
Statement of View	Only believers who are watching and waiting for the Lord will be raptured at various times before and during the 7-year Tribulation. Those who will be raptured are spiritually mature saints, both dead and living (1Th 4:13-18).
Proponents	Joseph Seiss, G. H. Lang, Robert Govett, Witness Lee, G. H. Pember, Ira E. David, D. H. Panton

Arguments For	Arguments Against
The New Testament often views the Resurrection as a reward to be strived for (Mt 19:28-29; Lk 9:62; 20:35; Php 3:10-14; Rev 2:11; 3:5). Therefore, not all believers will gain the first resurrection, only those who are worthy.	Rapture is part of the culmination of salvation. God starts salvation by grace and will finish it by grace, not by our works (Eph 2:8-9).
Other Scriptures indicate partial rapture of believers, or an idea similar to this (Mt 24:40-51).	There is confusion between verses that apply to Israel and verses that apply to the church in the gospel passages. This is not the Rapture, but a taking away to judgment as in the example of the Flood in Mt 24:39. 1Co 15:51-52 says all believers will be raptured.
The emphasis is on watching, waiting, working, and the hope of rewards (Mt 24:41-42; 25:1 13; 1Th 5:6; Heb 9:28).	The emphasis is on working for rewards (crowns, 2Ti 4:8) not for participation in the Rapture.
There are verses that emphasize the need to suffer in order to reign (Ro 8:16-17; Lk 22:28-30; Acts 14:22; Col 3:24; 2Th 1:4-5). Therefore, believers must suffer now or during the Tribulation before they can reign with Christ.	Believers suffer in every age, and all believers will reign with Christ. The suffering and reigning of Christians is never linked to any supposed order of the Rapture.
A believer, through sinning, can lose his right to enjoy the first resurrection and the kingdom (1Co 6:19-20; Gal 5:19-21; Heb 12:14).	These passages speak of the unsaved not entering the kingdom. They do not apply to believers.
Worthy, watching believers will be rewarded by being raptured before the Tribulation (Rev 3:10).	There is a division in the church, the body of Christ. It seems that those worthy of being translated will be raptured, while those not worthy will be left behind. Passages like Jn 14:1 and 1Co 15:51-52 obviously include all believers.
Since the baptism of the Spirit empowers to witness (Ac 1:8) and not all believers witness, not all believers are in the body of Christ (1Co 12: 13) and not all are raptured.	The baptism of the Spirit places all believers in the body of Christ (1Co 12:13).

Chart 52—*Views on the Rapture (Cont.)*

PREWRATH	
Statement of View	The tribulation period is divided into three stages found in the Olivet Discourse: (1) the beginning of sorrows (Mt 24:8), (2) the Great Tribulation (Mt 24: 21), and (3) the Day of the Lord (Mt 24:30-31). The Rapture takes place between the Great Tribulation and the Day of the Lord, and the Day of the Lord is the time when God will release his wrath.
Proponents	Marvin Rosenthal, Robert Van Kampen

Arguments For	Arguments Against
Wrath is limited to the Day of the Lord. It first appears in the text of Rev 6:16 following the opening of the sixth seal. The verb translated "is come" is aorist, thus it doesn't refer to the previous seals.	Wrath is evident throughout the entire tribulation period (Lk 21:21ff.) The Olivet Discourse is used to the exclusion of other evidence.
There is no blessing in the Day of the Lord (pp.127-28).* All of the biblical citations describe it negatively (Isa 2:19, 22; Joel 1:15; Zep 1:15; Zec 14:3; Ob 15; Eze 30:3; etc.).	There is blessing in the Day of the Lord. Joel 2:30ff. describes the Day of the Lord (vv. 30-31), blessing of deliverance (v. 32), and restoration of Judah's and Jerusalem's fortunes (3:1, 17-8, 20-21). See also Zec 2:8-13a, 12:2-14:20, Isa 34-35, Hag 2:6ff.
2Pe 3 describes the final eschatological Day of the Lord in connection with the Second Coming. The Millennium can't be included in the Day of the Lord because it introduces blessing. The physical changes God will make to the earth are a renovation made to prepare for the Millennium. The pretribulationist must hold that there are two "Day" periods—one during the tribulation period and another following it.	The text indicates that the Day of the Lord extends beyond the tribulation period to cover the Millenium and the creation of the new heavens and new earth. The physical changes God will make are a destruction and replacement, not a mere renovation. Pretribulationists hold to one "Day" period. The prewrath position is a straw man not held by pretribulationists.
The Great Tribulation appears in the middle of Daniel's 70th Week. It began as a 3½-year period and has been shortened to an unknown length. This is derived from Mt 24:22, "If those days had not been cut short ...".	In Mt 24:22 we don't know what this time period is shortened from or its ending. A prewrath time scheme is assumed, and upon this is built the timing of the seal, bowl, and trumpet judgments. There is no practical difference between the Great Tribulation and the Day of the Lord. Both are times of great suffering.
The five seals in Rev 6 are not "from God," because then God would be the author of sin. They are not signs of God's wrath on earth. The seals are neither under Christ's control nor are they events or containers of events. This view ascribes the works of the Antichrist to Christ. Revelation describes seals as representing the security of the believer, and does so in Rev 7.	A face value reading of the text shows that Christ (the Lamb) opens its seals. As the seals are opened, events take place. His opening of the seals shows Jesus to be in control of the events. God is using people and angels to accomplish his ends. If seals were the believer's security, then when they are broken, so is that security. The seventh seal arbitrarily becomes a container of events. It is also transformed into a symbol of judgment, not security.
The cosmic disturbances that are a result of the opening of the sixth seal are a precursor to the Day of the Lord.	The phenomena of Joel 2:31 are said to occur after, not before, the Day of the Lord starts. This appears in Joel 3:15, after the judgment of the nations in v. 12. Isa 2:19-21 tells of the rocks falling, which the prewrath position places before the Day of the Lord; but in the context of Isaiah, they fall during the Day of the Lord. The aorist verb, *elthen*, in the context of revelation referred to above, speaks of either a present or past event in contrast to Rosenthal's future view, (pp.167, 180).† His argument is by assertion not evidence.

*Page numbers cited are from Rosenthal.   †Page numbers cited are from Karleen.

Sources: Marvin Rosenthal, *The Prewrath Rapture of the Church* (Nashville: Thomas Nelson, 1990) and Paul S. Karleen, *The Prewrath Rapture of the Church, Is It Biblical?* (Langhorne, PA: BF Press, 1991).

Chart 52—*Views on the Rapture (Cont.)*

MIDTRIBULATION	
Statement of View	The church, believers in Christ, are raptured in the middle of the tribulation period, prior to the Great Tribulation. This view offers the best of the pretribulation and posttribulation positions. It also has a mid–Seventieth-Week Rapture.
Proponents	Gleason L. Archer, Norman Harrison, J. Oliver Buswell, Merrill C. Tenney, G. H. Lang

Arguments For	Arguments Against
This position offers fewer problems than either the pre- or posttribulational views. It avoids the problems of the two extremes.	There is a loss of imminency in this position (as also in posttribulation). No longer are we called upon to wait and watch but instead to look for preparatory signs, as given in the book of Revelation and in Mt 24:1-14.
Great emphasis is on the 3½ years (42 months, 1,260 days) in the Scripture, to divide the 7 years of Tribulation (Da 7; 9:27; 12:7; Rev 11:23; 12:3, 6, 14).	The emphasis on the middle of the Tribulation is due to the breaking of the covenant with Israel (Da 9:27), not because of the Rapture.
The Olivet Discourse (Mt 24-25) talks of the coming, appearance, and return of Christ. It coincides with the Rapture passage in 1Th 4:15.	The only concrete link between the Olivet Discourse and the return of Christ is the use of *parousia* in both passages. Many other differences in the contexts make this a weak link.
2Th 2:1-4 clearly specifies signs preceding the Rapture.	2Th 2:1-4. refers to the two events preceding the Day of the Lord, not the rapture of the church.
Rev 11:15-19 mentions the seventh trumpet, which is identical to the trumpet of God in 1Th 4:16.	Does the Rapture truly occur in Rev 11, just because there is a trumpet sound? The argument is weak and has no biblical basis.
This position keeps the distinction between the Rapture and the Revelation, thus, two stages in the coming of Christ.	Pretribulation also maintains temporal distinction. Posttribulation maintains a distinction as well, though it is a difference in essence rather than in time.
The church is delivered from the wrath of God but not from trials and testing since the Rapture occurs in the middle of the Tribulation, just prior to the great outpouring of God's wrath.	Those who hold this view must devise a new concept of wrath in the book of Revelation. There is a forced spiritualization of chaps. 1-11 for contemporary purposes, not future fulfillment. The church can be delivered from wrath either by pretribulation rapture or by protection from wrath.
Just as there is overlapping in the book of Acts in terms of the program of God for the church and Israel, so there is overlapping in the program of God in the book of Revelation.	The church has both Jews and Gentiles in it. This does not necessitate, however, an overlapping of God's program for the church and for national Israel.
This view allows for the nonglorified saints at the end of the Tribulation to enter the millennial kingdom to repopulate the world.	Pretribulation also allows for repopulation. Also, it is possible that some unbelievers will enter the Millennium since the conversion of Israel will not take place until the Second Advent.

Chart 52—*Views on the Rapture (Cont.)*

POSTTRIBULATION

Statement of View	Living believers are to be raptured at the second coming of Christ, which will occur at the end of the Tribulation. There are four views within this camp, categorized by Walvoord as: (1) classic, (2) semiclassic, (3) futurist, and (4) dispensational. The spectrum is broad, encompassing a period of time from the early church fathers to the present century.
Proponents	Classic: J. Barton Payne Semiclassic: Alexander Reese, Norman MacPherson, George L. Rose, George H. Fromow Futurist: George Ladd, Dave MacPherson Dispensational: Robert H. Gundry, Douglas J. Moo Others: Harold Ockenga, J. Sidlow Baxter

Arguments For	**Arguments Against**
The Rapture is preceded by unmistakable signs (Mt 24:3-31). These signs are part of the tribulation period the saints must go through. The culmination will be the return of Christ, which involves the rapture of believers (Mt 24:29-31, 40-41). In the Olivet Discourse Christ talks of the Rapture with the Revelation.	Posttribulation raises problems about the repopulation of the millennial kingdom by flesh-and-blood believers if they are all raptured and glorified.
The parable of the wheat and tares (Mt 13:24) shows that separation takes place at the end of the age. At that time the good (believers) are distinguished from the bad (unbelievers), and this occurs at the end of the Tribulation.	The view that the 144,000 in Revelation are the ones who populate the earth fails to take into consideration the context of this passage.
The order of resurrection demands that all believers of all ages be brought back in their glorified bodies at the end of the Tribulation (Rev 20:4-6).	The exegetical argument of Rev 3:10 with *ek* ("from") is weak. To interpret "trial" as anything else but God's wrath is not doing justice to this word or to the text.
The New Testament words on the return of Christ make no distinction of stages: epiphany, manifestation, revelation, parousia, the day, that day, the Day of Jesus Christ, the Day of the Lord Jesus, and the Day of the Lord.	The sequence of events, connecting 1Th 4 with the Rapture and 1Th 5 with the Day of the Lord, is glossed over in determining the chronological order of events.
The phrase "keep you from the hour of trial" in Rev 3:10 can also refer to deliverance from the wrath of Satan as it operates in the tribulation period.	Just as Scripture may be somewhat silent regarding a pretribulation rapture, so there is greater silence in a posttribulation rapture. This is especially true in John's prophetic letter of Revelation, where there is more emphasis on the return of Christ. A case in point is the vague mention of the church in Rev 4-18.
A rise in apostasy is a sign that will precede the return of Christ (2Th 2:8).	The argument that a posttribulation rapture was the belief of the historic Christian church falls apart when we see that what was believed in the early church is quite different from what is believed today. Nevertheless, the basis of doctrinal truth is not the early church, but the Word of God.
Much of scriptural teaching to the church concerning the end times is meaningless if the church does not go through the Tribulation (Mt 24:15-20).	This position conflicts with the teaching of the imminent return of Christ. Scripture teaches us to wait and watch, not for preparatory signs of Christ's coming, but for the blessed hope of his return (Tit 2:13).

53. A Survey of the Second Coming

Procedure

Public, visible revelation in power and glory (Mt 16:27; 26:64; Ac 1:9, 11; Rev 19:11-16)

Like a thief, but seen worldwide (from east to west) (Lk 21:34-35; 1Th 5:2-3; Mt 24:26-27; Rev 1:7)

Accompanied by divine glory, angelic hosts, and saints (Zec 14:5; Mt 16:27; 25:31; Jude 14; 1Th 3:13; 4:14; 2Th 1:7; Col 3:4)

With the voice of the archangel (1Th 4:16-17)

Riding a white horse (Rev 19:11)

Purpose

To reveal and glorify Christ (Zec 14:5; Col 3:4; 1Th 3:13; 2Th 1:10)

To conquer the Antichrist, False Prophet, and rebellious Gentile nations (Ps 2; 2Th 2:8; Rev 19:19-21)

To bind Satan and fallen angels (Rev 20:1-2)

To rescue and regenerate national Israel (Zec 14:3-4; Joel 3:15-16; Ac 3:19-21; 15:16)

To judge rebel Jews and the Gentile nations (Isa 24:21-23; Eze 20:33-38; Joel 3:1-2, 12; Mt 24:31-32; 2Th 1:7-9)

To establish the millennial kingdom (Zec 14:9; Da 7:13-14; Mt 25:31; Lk 21:27, 31; 2Ti 4:1)

To deliver the created order (Isa 11:6-9; Ro 8:19-22)

To establish universal peace and reward the Tribulation saints (Mt 16:27; 25:34; Mic 4:3-4; Isa 2:4)

Perspective

Witness for Christ (Lk 9:26)

Live a holy life (Tit 2:12, 14; 2Pe 3:11)

Be faithful in service (Mt 24:44-51; 1Pe 5:1-4)

Exercise self-control (Lk 21:35-36; Ac 24:25; Ro 13:13)

Work while it is day (Lk 19:13; Ro 13:11-12)

Look and wait for Christ (1Th 1:10; Tit 2:13)

Be patient with all men (Php 4:5; Heb 10:36-38; Jas 5:7-9)

Be alert and watchful (Mt 24:42, 44; 1Th 5:6)

Pray for soon coming (Rev 22:20)

Do not let your heart be troubled (Jn 14:1-3)

Do not judge fellow saints (1Co 4:5)

54. Reasons for Christ's Second Coming

Reason	Scripture Reference
1. To defeat the Antichrist and the world's nations assembled at Armageddon	Rev 19:17-21
2. To regather, regenerate, and restore faithful Israel	Isa 43:5-6 Jer 24:6 Eze 11:17; 36:28 Am 9:14-15 Mic 7:18-19 Mt 24:31
3. To judge and punish faithless Israel	Eze 11:21; 20:38
4. To separate the sheep from the goats	Mt 25:31-46
5. To resurrect Old Testament and Tribulation saints	Job 19:25-26 Ps 49:15 Isa 25:8; 26:19 Da 12:2 Hos 13:14 Jn 5:28-29 Heb 11:35 Rev 20:4-5
6. To judge fallen angels	1Co 6:3

List compiled by Harold Willmington. Used by permission.

55. Signs Suggesting the Return of Christ

Sign	Reference
1. Increase of wars and rumors of wars	Mk 13:7
2. Extreme materialism	2Ti 3:1-2
3. Lawlessness	2Ti 3:2-4
4. Population explosion	Ge 6:1 Lk 17:26
5. An increase in speed and knowledge	Da 12:4
6. Unification of the world's systems	Rev 13:4-8 Ps 2:1-3
7. Intense demonic activity	1Ti 4:1-3
8. A departure from the Christian faith	2Th 2:3 1Ti 4:1 2Ti 4:3-4 2Pe 3:3-4
9. Abnormal sexual activities	Lk 17:26, 28 2Pe 2:5-8
10. The abortion movement (Especially note the three words, "without natural affection," which can be accurately applied to mothers who murder their unborn children.)	2Ti 3:1–3 (KJV)

List compiled by Harold Willmington. Used by permission.

56. Second Coming Terminology

Revelation (ἀποκάλυψις–*apokalypsis*)	Advent (παρουσία–*parousia*)	Appearance (ἐπιφάνεια–*epiphaneia*)
Meaning: ἀπό ("away from") + καλύπτω ("to cover, hide"); "unveiling, revelation"	**Meaning:** "presence, coming, appearing, arrival"	**Meaning:** "to shine upon, bring forth into the light; manifestation, appearance"
Identified with the end of the age (1Co 1:1-8) and the day of God's wrath and righteous judgment (Ro 2:5)	Visible appearance in glory, like lightning shining from the east to the west (Mt 24:27)	Used for both First and Second Advents, although 6 of 10 NT uses are of Second Advent; used interchangeably with *parousia* ("advent"), with emphasis on visible appearance, e.g., "brightness" (2Th 2:8)
Brings rescue and relief to saints suffering tribulation (2Th 1:7)	Brings both dead and living saints to Christ in the air (1Th 4:15)	Brings reward to the saints who have loved Christ's "appearance" (2Ti 4:8)
Will include both Christ and angelic army in flaming fire and in vengeance (2Th 1:7-8, 10)	Will bring destructive judgment upon "the lawless one," the Antichrist (2Th 2:8)	Also brings destructive judgment upon "the lawless one," the Antichrist (2Th 2:8)
Time of the validation of the saints' faith (1Pe 1:7) and the vindication of their suffering (1Pe 4:13)	Time of rejoicing over the fruits of faithful ministry (1Th 2:19)	Time that ends saints' faithful confession of Christ before the world (1Ti 6:14)
Delivers created order from the curse of corruption and brings bodily redemption to saints (Ro 8:19-23)	Brings the resurrection of believers (1Co 15:23; 1Th 4:15)	Ushers in the kingdom (2Ti 4:1)
Incentive for holy life and diligent work for the Lord (1Co 1:7)	Incentive for present patience, confidence, and disciplined holy life (Jas 5:7-8; 1Jn 2:28; 2Th 2:1; 1Th 3:13; 5:23; 2Pe 3:11-12)	Incentive for self-denial and righteous life in present age (Tit 2:11-13)
Used of the message in the book of Revelation, which emphasizes the revelation of Christ's glory (Rev 1:1)	Promised event ridiculed by people in the last days (2Pe 3:3-4), upon whom it will come unexpectedly (Mt 24:37-39)	Used to translate "terrible," with reference to the "great and terrible Day of the Lord" (Ac 2:20 after LXX of Joel 2:31)

57. Contrasts between the Rapture Views

	Pretribulation	Midtribulation	Posttribulation	Partial Rapture	Prewrath
Time of Christ's coming in Relation to the Tribulation	Before	Midpoint	After	Before, during, and after	5½-year (66-month) point
Stages/Phases of the Second Coming	2	2	1	Many	2
Time Interval between the Stages	>7 years	<3½ years	Momentary	<=1,007 years	18 months
Divisions in the Tribulation Period	2	2	1 (?)	Individually based	3
Rapture Imminent?	Yes	No	No	"Yes"	No
Rapture Signs?	No	Yes	Yes	Depends	Yes
Length of Tribulation	7 years	3½ years	7 years	7 years	2 years
Length of *Great* Tribulation	7 (or 3½) years	3½ years (?)	7 years (?)	?	2 years
Length of Wrath	7 years	3½ years	7 years	7 years	18 months
Distinguishes Wrath from Tribulation?	No	No	No	No (?)	Yes
Rapture after Millennium?	No	No	No	Yes	No
Holy Spirit Present in Tribulation?	Absent (most) Present (some)	Present first 3½ years	Present 7 years	Present (?)	Present (?)
Believers (Church) Endure or Escape Purging?	All escape 7 years	All endure 3½ years and escape 3½ years	All endure 7 years	Faithful escape <=7 years; unfaithful endure <=7 years	All endure 5½ years
Key Passages Cited	Rev 3:10; 1Th 4:13-18	Da 9:27; 1Th 5:3	Lk 21:34-36; 2Th 1:6-10	Mt 24:41-42; Heb 9:28; 1Co 15:23	Rev 3:10
Affinity to Amillennial/ Postmillenial Position	None	None	Much	None	None
Theological Perspective	Dispensational premillennialism	"Undefined" premillennialism	Covenant premillennialism	"Undefined" premillennialism	"Undefined" premillennialism
Advocates	Benware, Feinberg, Hoyt, Lightner, Ludwigson, Pentecost, Ryrie, Thiessen, Walvoord, Wood	Archer, Buswell, N. Harrison, W. Harrison	Grudem, Gundry, Ladd, McPherson, Moo, Mounce, Reese	Govett, Lang, Witness Lee, Panton, Pember, Seiss, Sparks, Waugh	Rosenthal, Van Kampen

58. Contrasts between the Rapture and the Revelation

> "Looking for the blessed hope *and* the appearing of the glory of
> our great God and Savior, Christ Jesus" (Tit 3:13)

THE RAPTURE	THE REVELATION
1. A "mystery" truth revealed only in New Testament (1Co 15:51)	1. A central truth revealed in both testaments (Jude 14)
2. *Translation* of church age believers	2. *No translation* at all
3. *Pre*tribulational (Rev 3:10)	3. *Post*tribulational (Rev 19:11-21)
4. Christ comes in the *air* (1Th 4:16)	4. Christ comes to the *earth* (Zec 14:4, 9; Mt 25:31)
5. Christ comes *for* the saints (Jn 14:1-2; 1Th 4:15-17)	5. Christ comes *with* the saints (Mt 25:31-32; 1Th 3:13; Rev 19:14)
6. Translated saints go to *heaven* (Jn 14:2-3; 1Th 4:17)	6. Saints already on earth remain on *earth* to enter Kingdom (Mt 25:34; Rev 5:10)
7. Related to the *Church* (1Co 15:51-52; 1Th 4:16)	7. Related to *Israel* (Zec 14:2-3, 16; Mt 19:28; Ac 3:17-21)
8. Earth and nations *not judged*	8. Earth and nations *judged* (Rev 6-19)
9. *Imminent, signless* (1Co 15:52; 1Th 4:16)	9. *Not imminent;* follows *definite predicted signs* (Mt 24:29-31; Mk 13:14-26, 29; Ac 2:19-21; Rev 1:7; 6-19)
10. *Before* the day of wrath (Rev 3:10)	10. *Climaxes* the time of wrath (Rev 6:10; 19:11)
11. Affects only *believers* (Rev 3:10)	11. Affects *all humanity* (Mt 24:37-39; Rev 6:10)
12. *Invisible,* seen only by Church (1Th 1:9-10; 4:14-17)	12. *Visible,* seen by entire world (Rev 1:7; cf. Mt 24:27; Lk 21:27)
13. Fulfills promise of Jesus to the *Church* where Jew/Gentile distinctions do not exist (Jn 14:1-3; 1Th 4:15; cf. Eph 2:11-16)	13. Fulfills promise of God to *Israel* made in covenants (Ge 12:1-3; Ps 89; Isa 11:11-14; cf. Ro 11:26-27)

Chart 58—*Contrasts between the Rapture and the Revelation (Cont.)*

14. *Church* saints are delivered *from* this world (1Th 1:10; 5:9; Rev 3:10)	14. *Jewish* saints are delivered *in* this world (Jer 30:17; Zec 14:3-5; Lk 21:28)
15. *Announced* by an archangel (1Th 4:16)	15. *Attended* by myriads of angels (Mt 24:31; 25:31; Jude 14)
16. *Church* is removed (1Th 4:13-18)	16. *Satan* is removed (Rev 20:1-3)
17. Evil begins to *increase* (2Th 2:1-12)	17. Evil is *suppressed* (2Th 1:7; Ps 37:9-10)
18. Primary purpose is *salvation of believers* from coming wrath (1Th 1:10)	18. Primary purpose is *judgment of unbelievers* by present wrath (Mt 25:31–46; Rev 11:18; 19:15)
19. *No reference* to Satan or Antichrist	19. Satan bound; Antichrist judged (Rev 19:20; 20:1-3)
20. Judgment seat of Christ for *Church in heaven* (2Co 5:10; 1Co 3:13)	20. Judgment of Jews and Gentiles to enter *Kingdom on earth* (Eze 20:34; Mt 25:32)
21. Jesus demonstrated to be *Head of the Church* (Eph 1:10, 22; 4:15; Col 1:18; 2:10)	21. Jesus vindicated as *Messianic King to Israel* (Zec 14:3-4, 9; cf. Ac 1:6, 11)
22. Ushers in *Tribulation* (Rev 3:10)	22. Ushers in *Millennial Kingdom* (Mt 24:31; 1Co 15:23)
23. The *Lord* is at hand (Php 4:5)	23. The *Kingdom* is at hand (Mt 24:14)
24. Bodies of Church saints made *immortal* (1Co 15:50-57; Php 3:20-21) and taken to heaven for 7 years (1Th 4:17)	24. Bodies of Tribulation saints left in *mortal state* to live on earth for 1,000 years (Mt 25:31-34)
25. Nature is subsequently *ruined* (Rev 6-19)	25. Nature is subsequently *restored* (Isa 11:6-9; Ro 8:19-22)
26. Produces comfort, hope, patience, and purity (1Th 4:18; Tit 2:13; 1Th 1:10; 1Jn 3:3)	26. Produces fear and judgment (Mt 24:27-31; Lk 21:20-28; Rev 6:16-17)
27. Prophecies (concerning Israel) *yet* to be fulfilled	27. *All* prophecies (concerning Israel) fulfilled
28. *Preparation* for the Day of the Lord (2Th 2:2-8)	28. *Part* of the Day of the Lord (2Pe 3:10-13)
29. Living and dead church age saints are resurrected (1Th 4:13-17)	29. Saints and sinners are both resurrected, though separated by 1,000 years (Rev 20:4-5)
30. Judgment follows for *heavenly rewards* (2Co 5:10; cf. 1Co 3:11-15)	30. Judgment follows for *punishment in Lake of Fire* (Rev 20:11-15)

59. A Graphic Look at Views on the Time of the Rapture

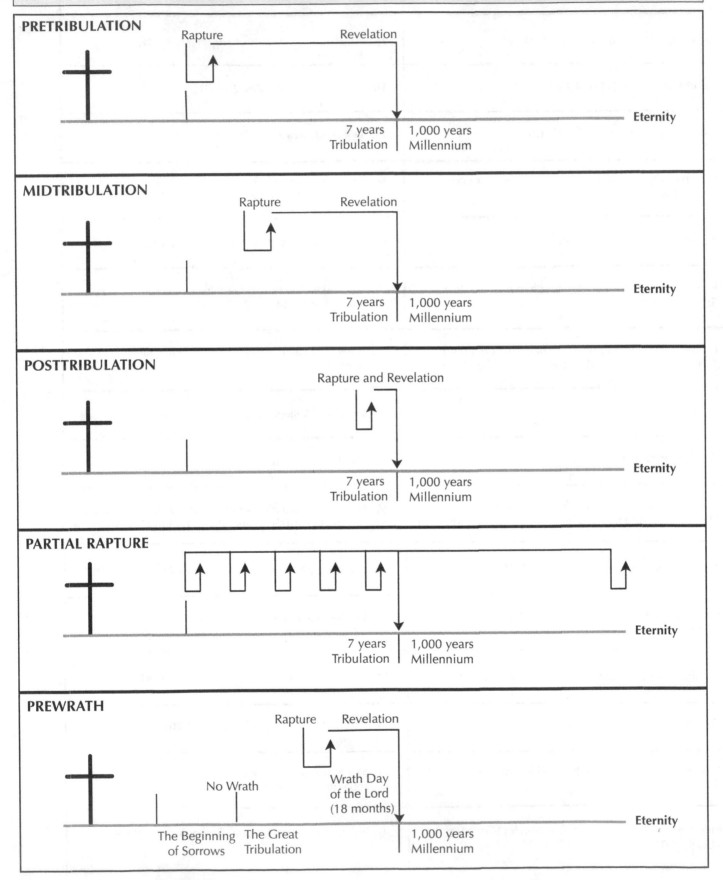

PRETRIBULATION

Rapture   Revelation

7 years Tribulation | 1,000 years Millennium   Eternity

MIDTRIBULATION

Rapture   Revelation

7 years Tribulation | 1,000 years Millennium   Eternity

POSTTRIBULATION

Rapture and Revelation

7 years Tribulation | 1,000 years Millennium   Eternity

PARTIAL RAPTURE

7 years Tribulation | 1,000 years Millennium   Eternity

PREWRATH

Rapture   Revelation

No Wrath

Wrath Day of the Lord (18 months)   Eternity

The Beginning of Sorrows   The Great Tribulation   1,000 years Millennium

60. The Pretrib Rapture Doctrine

Pretrib Rapture

- Nature of the Tribulation
- Nature of the Church
- Doctrine of Imminency
- Work of the Holy Spirit
- Interval Needed Between Comings
- Contrasts Between Comings

Distinction Between Israel and Church

Futurism

Premillennialism

Literal Interpretation

FOUNDATIONAL SUPPORT

Diagram from Thomas Ice, *Bible Prophecy Charts* (Arlington, TX: The Pre-Trib Research Center, n.d.). Used by permission.

PART 7

The Nation of Israel

61. The Sacred Sanctuary in History and Prophecy

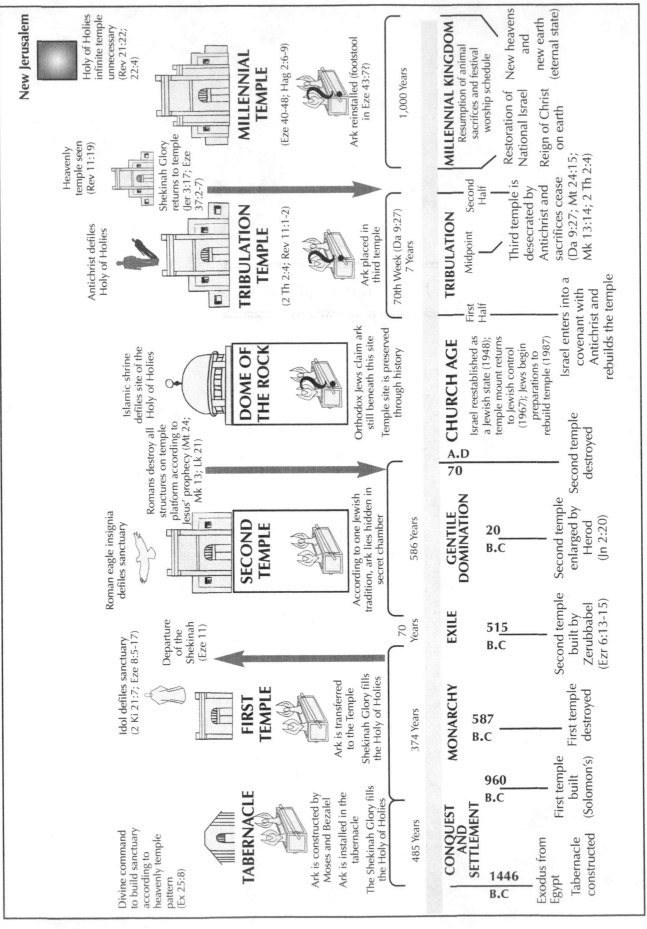

New Jerusalem

Holy of Holies infinite temple unnecessary (Rev 21:22; 22:4)

MILLENNIAL TEMPLE

Heavenly temple seen (Rev 11:19)

Shekinah Glory returns to temple (Jer 3:17; Eze 37:2-7)

(Eze 40-48; Hag 2:6-9)

Ark reinstalled (footstool in Eze 43:7?)

1,000 Years

TRIBULATION TEMPLE

Antichrist defiles Holy of Holies

(2 Th 2:4; Rev 11:1-2)

Ark placed in third temple

70th Week (Da 9:27) 7 Years

Islamic shrine defiles site of the Holy of Holies

DOME OF THE ROCK

Romans destroy all structures on temple platform according to Jesus' prophecy (Mt 24; Mk 13; Lk 21)

Roman eagle insignia defiles sanctuary

Orthodox Jews claim ark still beneath this site
Temple site is preserved through history

SECOND TEMPLE

According to one Jewish tradition, ark lies hidden in secret chamber

586 Years

Idol defiles sanctuary (2 Ki 21:7; Eze 8:5-17)

Departure of the Shekinah (Eze 11)

FIRST TEMPLE

Ark is transferred to the Temple
Shekinah Glory fills the Holy of Holies

374 Years

70 Years

Divine command to build sanctuary according to heavenly temple pattern (Ex 25:8)

TABERNACLE

Ark is constructed by Moses and Bezalel
Ark is installed in the tabernacle
The Shekinah Glory fills the Holy of Holies

485 Years

CONQUEST AND SETTLEMENT	MONARCHY	EXILE	GENTILE DOMINATION	CHURCH AGE	TRIBULATION	MILLENNIAL KINGDOM
1446 B.C	960 B.C / 587 B.C	515 B.C	20 B.C / A.D 70		First Half / Midpoint / Second Half	Restoration of National Israel / Reign of Christ on earth / Resumption of animal sacrifices and festival worship schedule / New heavens and new earth (eternal state)

Exodus from Egypt
Tabernacle constructed

First temple built (Solomon's)

First temple destroyed

Second temple built by Zerubbabel (Ezr 6:13-15)

Second temple enlarged by Herod (Jn 2:20)

Second temple destroyed

Israel reestablished as a Jewish state (1948); temple mount returns to Jewish control (1967); Jews begin preparations to rebuild temple (1987)

Israel enters into a covenant with Antichrist and rebuilds the temple

Third temple is desecrated by Antichrist and sacrifices cease (Da 9:27; Mt 24:15; Mk 13:14; 2 Th 2:4)

62. Prophetic Significance of Israel's Annual Feasts

"The seven appointed times were given as a typical presentation of the commitments made to Israel in the Abrahamic Covenant and those which amplified it. As these can be fulfilled only by Israel, so the typology of the feasts can relate only to that nation."*

	FIRST ADVENT OF CHRIST — Spring Cycle				SECOND ADVENT OF CHRIST — Fall Cycle		
FEAST	*Passover*	*Unleavened Bread*	*First Fruits*	*Weeks (Pentecost)*	*Trumpets*	*Day of Atonement*	*Tabernacles*
Jewish Calendar	14th day of Nisan	15th–21st day of Nisan	16th day of Nisan	50 days after First Fruits	1st day of Tishri	10th day of Tishri	15th–21st day of Tishri
Western Calendar	March–April	March–April	March–April	May–June	September–October	September–October	September–October
Biblical Reference	Ex 12; Lev 23:5	Lev 23:6-8; Nu 28:17	Lev 23:9-14	Lev 23:9-14	Lev 23:25; Nu 21:1-6	Lev 16; 23:26-32; Nu 27:7-11	Lev 23:33-43; Nu 21:12-38
Occasion for Feast	Remembrance of redemption	Remembrance of separation	Expectation of full harvest	Appropriation of God's supply	Preparation for national repentance	Cleansing of national sin	Remembrance of God's provision
Prophetic Time Period	Death of Messiah on cross at Passover	Death of Messiah on cross at Passover	Resurrection of Jesus	Giving of the Holy Spirit at birth of church	End of Tribulation at time of Gentile attack on Jerusalem	Second Advent (final battle of Armageddon)	Millennial kingdom
Typico-prophetic Significance/ Fulfillment of Feast	National redemption provided through prophesied sacrifice of Lamb of God	Separated life prescribed for national Israel made possible by provision of Messiah as the Bread of Life	Resurrection of Messiah as basis for expectation of future resurrection	Provision of Holy Spirit for national Israel under new covenant (to be realized in future in God's kingdom)	Preparation for national repentance (predicted at close of Daniel's 70th Week, to rescue and regather nation)	National repentance and spiritual cleansing effected by faith in Messiah's atonement	Fulfillment of Abrahamic covenant, including blessing for nations through Israel and provision of physical and spiritual rest in the Land
Prophetic Reference	Isa 53; Ps 22; 1Co 5:7	Dt 7:6; Jn 6:35; 1Co 10:16-17	Da 12:2-3; 1Co 15:20, 23	Ac 2:1-4; Jcel 2:28-32	Zec 12:1-9; Mt 24:31	Zec 12:10-13:1; Mt 24:30; Ro 11:27	Zec 14:16-19

*Quote and chart (adapted) from Terry C. Hulbert, "The Eschatological Significance of Israel's Annual Feasts" (Th.D. dissertation, Dallas Theological Seminary, 1965).

PART 7: THE NATION OF ISRAEL

63. Prophetic Significance of Old Testament Offerings

Name	Translation	Major Reference	Distinctiveness	Symbolism	Typology
"Sweet Savor" Offerings					
Ola	Burnt offering	Lev 1; 6:8-13	Wholly burned on the altar (Lev 1:9)	1. Placating the wrath of God by substituting a victim in death (Ge 8:20; Lev 1:4) 2. Complete consecration (cf. Lev 6:13, a continual offering)	1. Christ's vicarious death for the redemption of sinners (2Co 5:21)
Minha	Meal offering	Lev 2; 6:14-23	Nonblood products, accompanying other blood offerings (Lev 2:1, cf. 23:18)	Consecration of one's life and substance (Lev 2:14)	Christ's righteous fulfilling of the law (Mt 3:15)
Sh'lamin	Peace offering	Lev 3; 7:11-34	Most parts eaten before God by the sacrificer (Lev 7:15)	1. Placating God's wrath (as above; cf. Lev 3:2) 2. A thanksgiving meal of reconciliation with God (Lev 7:12)	1. Vicarious redemption (as above) 2. Communion in Christ, now (Jn 6:51) and in the future kingdom (Rev 19:6-10)
Guilt Offerings					
Hattath	Sin offering	Lev 4-5:13; 6:24-30	For a specific sin (Lev 5:1-4) Some bodies of sacrifices burned outside the camp (Lev 4:12)	1. Placating God's wrath (as above; cf. 4:4) 2. Confession (Lev 5:5), with transference of guilt to the animal (Lev 4:21)	1. Vicarious redemption (as above) 2. Christ's suffering "outside the city gate" (Heb 13:12), the passive bearing of the penalties of men's sins (Isa 53:6)
Asham	Trespass offering	Lev 5:14-6:7; 7:1-10	Same as the Hattath, plus repayment to the wronged party (Lev 5:15)	1. Placating God's wrath (as above; cf. Lev 5:18) 2. Confession with transferred guilt (as above; Lev 7:7) 3. Social restitution for wrong (Lev 5:15)	Same as above (Isa 53:10), plus Christ's active redressing of every legal claim of God (Gal 4:4)

Chart adapted from Payne, *Encyclopedia of Biblical Prophecy*, 193.

64. The Temples of Israel in Islam

The Israelites (*Bani Isra'il*) 17:5-7	5 "So when of the two, the first warning came to pass, We raised against you Our servants, of mighty prowess, so they made havoc in (your) houses. And it was an accomplished threat. 6 Then We gave you back the turn against them, and aided you with wealth and children and made you a numerous band. 7 If you do good, you do good for your own souls. And if you do evil, it is for them. So when the second warning came, (We raised another people) that they might bring you to grief and that they might enter the Mosque as they entered it the first time, and that they might destroy, whatever they conquered, with utter destruction.	Commentary by Maulana Muhammad Ali: "V. 5 relates the destruction of the Temple at Jerusalem and the murder, imprisonment, and banishment of the Jews by the Babylonians in the year 588 B.C., while v. 6 relates to the return of the Jews and rebuilding of the Temple under Zerubabbel, and to their subsequent prosperity. This is the turn of fortune spoken of here." Speaking of v. 7: "This verse describes the destruction of the Temple a second time, which was accomplished by the Romans under Titus." Notes at bottom of Qur'anic text. *The Holy Qur'an,* 7th ed., rev., Arabic text, English translation and commentary by Maulana Muhammad Ali, (Columbus,Ohio: Ahmadiyyah Anjuman Isha'at Islam Lahore, Inc., 1917, 1991), 545. The understanding of two Jewish temples is confirmed by the Qur'an of Abdullah Yusuf Ali, published at the King Fahd Holy Qur'an Printing Complex in Medina, Saudi Arabia, by royal decree. It is generally considered the most orthodox Sunni translation and commentary. (We permitted your enemies) To disfigure your faces, And to enter your Temple As they had entered it before, And to visit with destruction All that fell into their power. The word that is translated "Temple" is the Arabic word *masjid,* usually translated "mosque," so the first translation above by Maulana Muhammad Ali. [Both the translation source and commment on *masjid* is given by Martin Kramer, "The Temples of Jerusalem in Islam," *Special Reports on the Arab-Israelit Peace Process,* no. 277, September 18, 2000, (Washington, D.C.: Washington Institute). http://www.mfa.gov.il/mfa/go.asp?MFAH0hz70]
The Saba' (*Al-Saba'*) 34:13	13 "They made for him what he pleased, of synagogues and images, and bowls (large) as watering-troughs and fixed cooking-pots. Give thanks, O people of David! And very few of My servants are grateful." 13 ["They worked for him As he desired, (making) Arches, Images, Basons As large as well, And (cooking) Cauldrons fixed (In their places)" Translation of Abdullah Yusuf Ali]	Muslim tradition is clear regarding the existence of the first temple, as revealed from this portion of the Qur'an in which Solomon, a prophet in Islamic thought, summons jinn or spirits to build the temple. Martin Kramer says, "Early Muslims regarded the building and destruction of the Temple of Solomon as a major historical and religious event, and accounts of the Temple are offered by many of the early Muslim historians and geographers (including Ibn Qutayba, Ibn al-Faqih, Mas'udi, Muhallabi, and Biruni)." Kramer, "The Temples of Jerusalem in Islam."

Chart 64—*The Temples of Israel in Islam (Cont.)*

The Israelites (*Bani Isra'il*) 17:1	1 "Glory to Him Who carried His servant by night from the Sacred Mosque to the Remote Mosque, whose precincts We blessed, that We might show him of Our signs! Surely He is the Hearing, the Seeing." 1 ["Glory to (Allah) Who did take His Servant For a Journey by night From the Sacred Mosque To the Farthest Mosque" Translation of Abdullah Yusuf Ali]	The Islamic view of Haram al-Sharif is based on 17:1. Maulana Muhammad Ali says of v. 1 in his notes: "The carrying by night of the Prophet from the Sacred Mosque at Makkah to the Remote Mosque at Jerusalem is in reference to the Prophets' reported Ascension." He continues: "*Isra'* is, in fact, the first stage in *Mi'raj,* as before his Ascension to heaven, the Prophet was taken to the Remote Mosque, or the Temple at Jerusalem. That the Ascension was not a translation of the body, but the spiritual experience of the Holy Prophet, as shown in 1441 under v. 60, where it is expressly called a *ru'ya,* or a *vision.* As the significance of the Ascension was the spiritual eminence of the Holy Prophet and indicated his triumph in the world, his being carried to the Temple at Jerusalem signified that he would also inherit the blessings of the Israelite prophets." *Special Reports on the Arab-Israeli Peace Process,* no. 277, September 18, 2000. No mosque stood in Jerusalem at the time of Muhammad, and the Muslims conquered the city several years after his death. The traditional explanation is offered by Abdullah Yusaf Ali in his commentary: "The Farthest Mosque must refer to the site of the Temple of Solomon in Jerusalem on the hill of Moriah." David, in Islamic teaching, was believed to have searched for a place of prayer (*musalla*), mentioned in 38:21, and chose the site for Solomon. Caliph Umar, when he visited Jerusalem, ordered a place of prayer to be built on Moriah, which came to be the Aqsa Mosque, south of the Dome of the Rock. Kramer, "The Temples of Jerusalem in Islam."

65. The Temple in the Messianic Redemptive Program for Israel and the Church

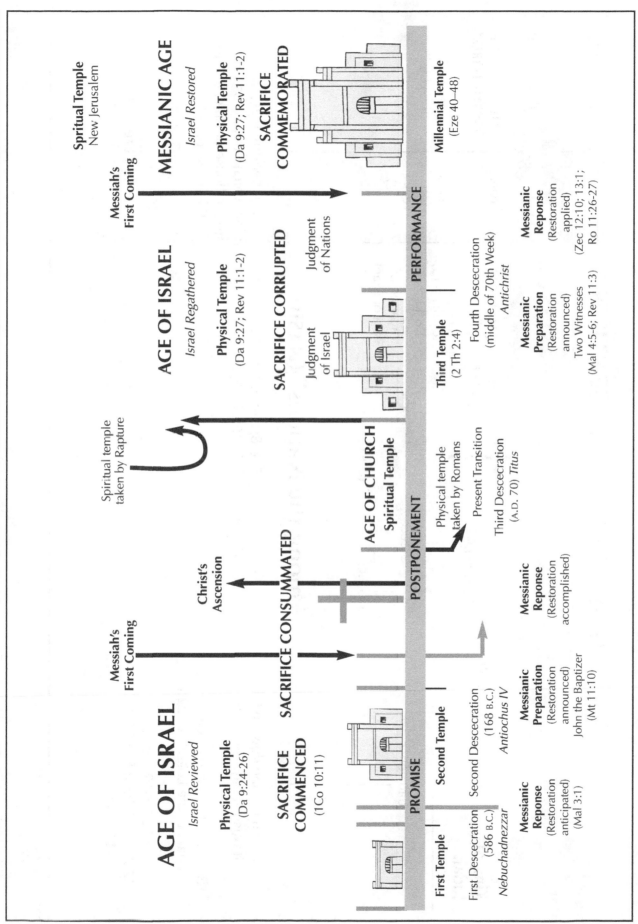

Compare the futurist perspective of this chart with that of the historicist in chart 46.

PART 7: THE NATION OF ISRAEL

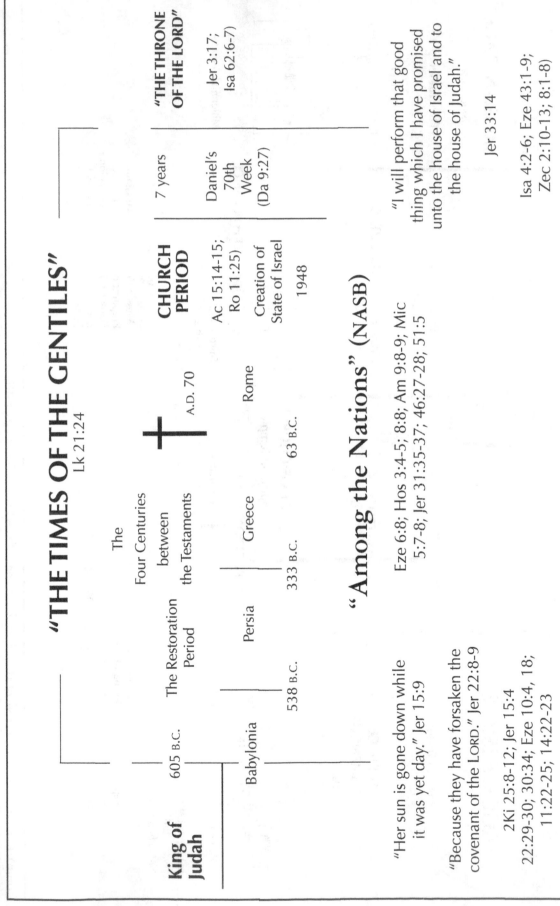

"THE TIMES OF THE GENTILES"
Lk 21:24

King of Judah

Babylonia

605 B.C.

538 B.C.

The Restoration Period

Persia

333 B.C.

Greece

63 B.C.

Rome

A.D. 70

CHURCH PERIOD

Ac 15:14-15; Ro 11:25)

Creation of State of Israel 1948

The Four Centuries between the Testaments

Daniel's 70th Week (Da 9:27)

7 years

"THE THRONE OF THE LORD"

Jer 3:17; Isa 62:6-7)

"I will perform that good thing which I have promised unto the house of Israel and to the house of Judah."

Jer 33:14

Isa 4:2-6; Eze 43:1-9; Zec 2:10-13; 8:1-8)

"Among the Nations" (NASB)

Eze 6:8; Hos 3:4-5; 8:8; Am 9:8-9; Mic 5:7-8; Jer 31:35-37; 46:27-28; 51:5

"Her sun is gone down while it was yet day." Jer 15:9

"Because they have forsaken the covenant of the LORD." Jer 22:8-9

2Ki 25:8-12; Jer 15:4
22:29-30; 30:34; Eze 10:4, 18;
11:22-25; 14:22-23

Scripture quotations are from KJV.

67. God's Covenant with Israel

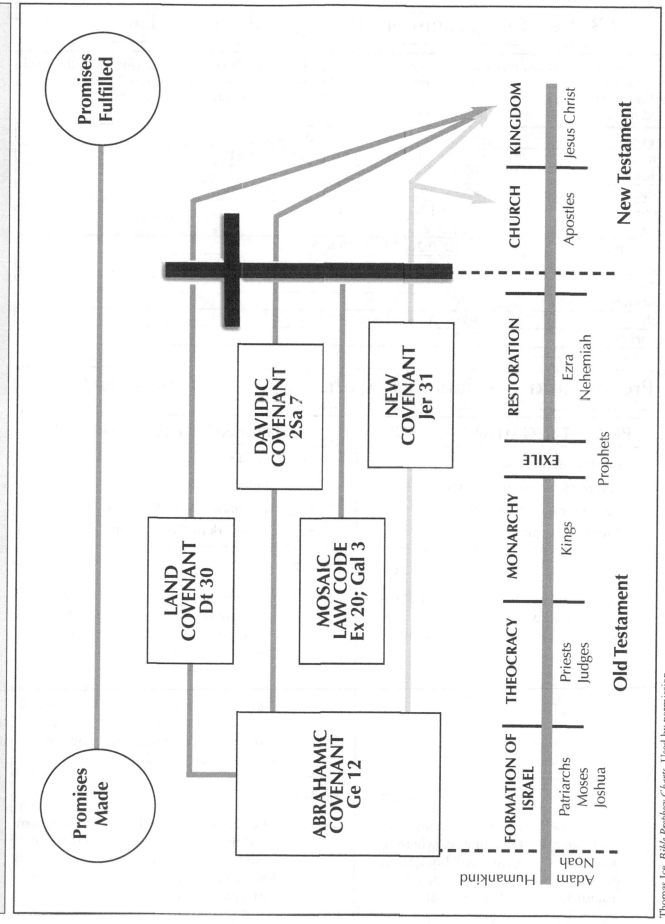

Promises Made

Promises Fulfilled

LAND COVENANT
Dt 30

DAVIDIC COVENANT
2Sa 7

MOSAIC LAW CODE
Ex 20; Gal 3

NEW COVENANT
Jer 31

ABRAHAMIC COVENANT
Ge 12

FORMATION OF ISRAEL | THEOCRACY | MONARCHY | EXILE | RESTORATION | CHURCH | KINGDOM

Adam
Noah
Patriarchs
Moses
Joshua

Priests
Judges

Kings

Prophets

Ezra
Nehemiah

Apostles

Jesus Christ

Humankind

Old Testament

New Testament

Thomas Ice, *Bible Prophecy Charts*. Used by permission.

PART 7: THE NATION OF ISRAEL

68. Key Old Testament Passages about the Land

Perhaps more than with any other religious group (including Christians), the heart of Judaism lies in the land of its forefathers. The land and the people are inseparable to Jews, for they experienced God's very presence indwelling the temple in Jerusalem for centuries (966-586 B.C.). This emphasis on the land of Canaan is repeated numerous times in the Old Testament.

Genesis	12:7; 13:14-17; 15:7-21; 17:1-8; 24:7; 28:13-15
Jeremiah	12:7; 13:14-17; 15:7-21; 17:1-8; 24:7; 28:13-15
Exodus	12:25; 13:5, 11; 32:13; 33:1
Ezekiel	11:17-21; 17:22-24; 34:11-31; 37:1-14
Numbers	11:12; 14:15-16, 23; 32:8
Hosea	13:9-14:9
Deuteronomy	1:8; 6:10; 9:28; 12:20; 19:8; 27:3
Micah	2:12
Joshua	23:5
Zephaniah	2:19-20
Isaiah	5:25-26; 11:11-12; 66:19-20
Zechariah	12:10-11

David Larsen, *Israel, Gentiles and the Church*, 269.

69. Present and Permanent Regathering in the Prophetic Books

PRESENT REGATHERING	PERMANENT REGATHERING
• Worldwide in its scope	• Worldwide in its extent
• Return to a part of the Land	• Return to all of the Land
• Restoration is to the Land	• Restoration is to the Lord
• The work of man (secular)	• The work of God (spiritual)

Ezekiel 36:24-27

Stage I: I will take you out of the nations; I will gather you from all the countries and bring you back into your own land (v. 24).	Stage II: I will sprinkle clean water on you, and you will be clean; I will cleanse you from all your impurities and from all your idols. I will give you a new heart and put a new spirit in you; I will remove from you your heart of stone and give you a heart of flesh. And I will put my Spirit in you and move you to follow my decrees and be careful to keep my laws (vv. 25-27).

Jeremiah 23:3-4

Stage I: I Myself will gather the remnant of My flock out of all the countries where I have driven them and will bring them back to their pasture, and they will be fruitful and multiply (v. 3 NASB).	Stage II: I will also raise up shepherds over them and they will tend them; and they will not be afraid any longer, nor be terrified, nor will any be missing (v. 4 NASB).

70. Israel's Two End-Time Regatherings to the Land

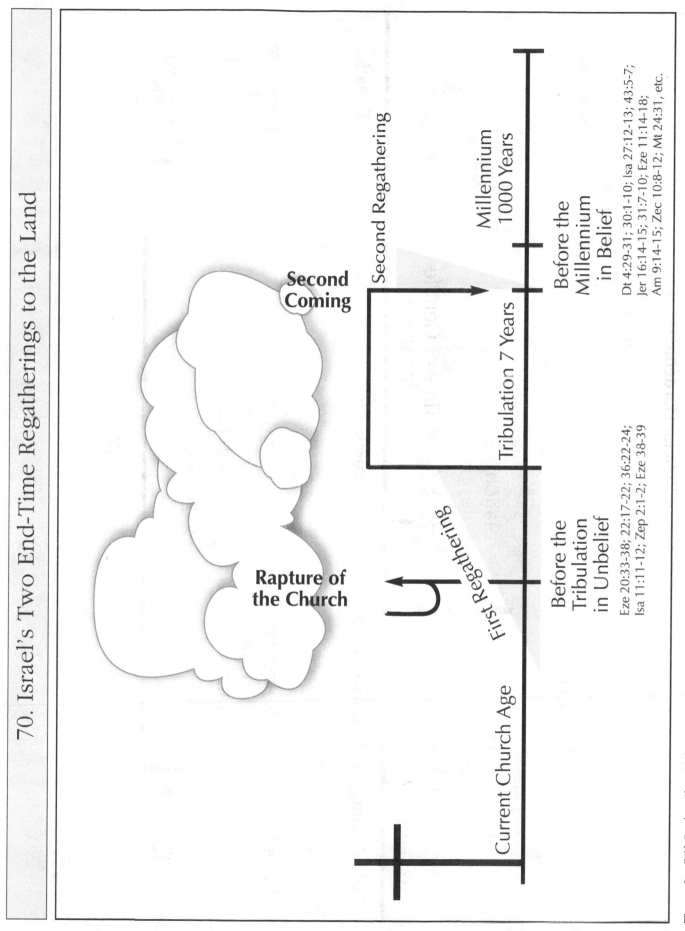

Second Coming

Second Regathering

Millennium
1000 Years

Before the
Millennium
in Belief

Dt 4:29-31; 30:1-10; Isa 27:12-13; 43:5-7;
Jer 16:14-15; 31:7-10; Eze 11:14-18;
Am 9:14-15; Zec 10:8-12; Mt 24:31, etc.

Tribulation 7 Years

First Regathering

**Rapture of
the Church**

Before the
Tribulation
in Unbelief

Eze 20:33-38; 22:17-22; 36:22-24;
Isa 11:11-12; Zep 2:1-2; Eze 38-39

Current Church Age

Thomas Ice, *Bible Prophecy Chart*, (Arlington, TX: The Pre-Trib Research Center, n.d.). Used by permission.

PART 7: THE NATION OF ISRAEL

Duration of Judicial Hardening

Ro 11:5; Eph 2:12-19

Coming of Christ

Near fulfillment of judgment
Desolation, exile
586 B.C.

740-680 B.C.

Coming of Christ

Far fulfillment of judgment
Desolation, exile
Zec 12-14

Mt 23:38-39
Desolation, exile
A.D. 70

Church Remnant Israel

Time of Gentile inclusion

Tribulation

Rejection by Israel concludes

Hardening ends
Ro 11:25b-27

Church Age

Ro 11:17, 24, 31

Rejection by Israel continues

Ac 28:24-28; Ro 11:25a, 28

Christ's time

Rejection by Israel culminates

Jn 12:38-41

Isaiah's time

Rejection by Israel condemned

Hardening begins
Isa 6:9-10

The Remnant

Isa 6:11-13; 10:20-22; Ro 9:27; 11:5

PART 8

Teaching on the Tribulation

72. Comparison of Tribulation Texts in the Old and New Testaments

Biblical Text	Dt 4	Jer 30	Da 9	Da 12	Mt 24/Mk 13	2Th 2	Rev 6-19
Event	Tribulation (*sar*) (v. 30)	Tribulation (*sar*) (v. 7)	seven-year covenant (v. 27a)	Tribulation (*sar*) (v. 1b)	Tribulation (*thlipsis*) (24:21; 13:19)	revealing of Antichrist (vv. 3, 8)	Great Tribulation (7:15)
Time reference	after previous exiles, latter days (v. 30)	great day, that day (vv. 7, 8)	70th week (v. 27)	end time (11:40)	those days, immediately prior to Second Advent (Mt 24: 22, 29)	Day of the Lord (v. 2), in his time [i.e., day of Antichrist] (v. 6)	great day of wrath (6:17), hour of judgment (14:7), great day of God (16:14)
Scope	has anything been done like this? [ref. to Exodus] (v. 32)	none like it (v. 7), complete destruction (v. 11)	complete destruction (v. 27c)	such as never occurred (v. 1)	such as never occurred nor ever shall (24:21; 13:19)	"bring to an end" [complete destruction] (v. 8)	such as had not been since man came on earth (16:18)
Religious context	idolatry (vv. 25, 28)	false prophets (29:24-32)	prince that will come (Antichrist), abomination of desolation (v. 27)	Antichrist (11:36-45), wicked (12:10)	false prophets' signs and wonders (24:24; 13:22)	Antichrist, false signs and wonders (vv. 4-9)	Antichrist, false prophets' signs and wonders (13:1-14)
Temple activity	promise of spiritual restoration (v. 30)	promise of spiritual restoration and theocracy (v. 9)	temple desecrated (v. 27)	temple desecrated (v. 11)	temple desecrated (24:15; 13:14)	temple desecrated (v. 4)	temple desecrated (11:1, 2)
Salvation message	you will return (v. 30)	saved from time (v. 7)	implied in destruction of desolator (v. 27)	[elect] rescued (v. 1)	elect saved (24:22; 13:20)	day will not come [upon you], elect saved (vv. 3, 13)	bondservants of God saved (19:1, 2)

73. Biblical Purposes for the Tribulation

Note that these purposes relate specifically to Israel.

Purpose	Reference
To complete the decreed period of national Israel's judicial hardening as punishment for her rejection of the messianic program, which the partial return from exile did not remove and which culminated in the national rejection of Jesus	Isa 6:9-13; 24:1-6; cf. Jn 12:37-41; Ro 11:7-10
To produce a messianic revival among Jewish people scattered throughout the world	Dt 4:27-30; cf. Rev 7:1-4; Mt 24:14
To convince the Jewish nation of their need for the Messiah to produce a national regeneration	Da 12:5-7; Jer 31:31-34; Eze 20:34-38; 36:25-27; 37:1-14; Zec 12:9-13:2; Isa 59:20-21
To provoke a complete return of world Jewry to the Land of Israel	Zec 8:7-8; Eze 36:24; 37:21
To end the Time of the Gentiles and effect the deliverance of the Jewish people from Gentile dominion	Isa 24:21-23; 59:16-20; cf. Mt 24:29-31; Mk 13:24-27; Ro 11:25
To purge the earth of wicked people (including rebel Jews and oppressive Gentiles) in order to establish the messianic kingdom in righteousness	Isa 11:9; 13:9; 24:19-20; Eze 20:33-38; 37:23; Zec 13:2; 14:9; Mt 25:31-46

74. Major Events of the Tribulation

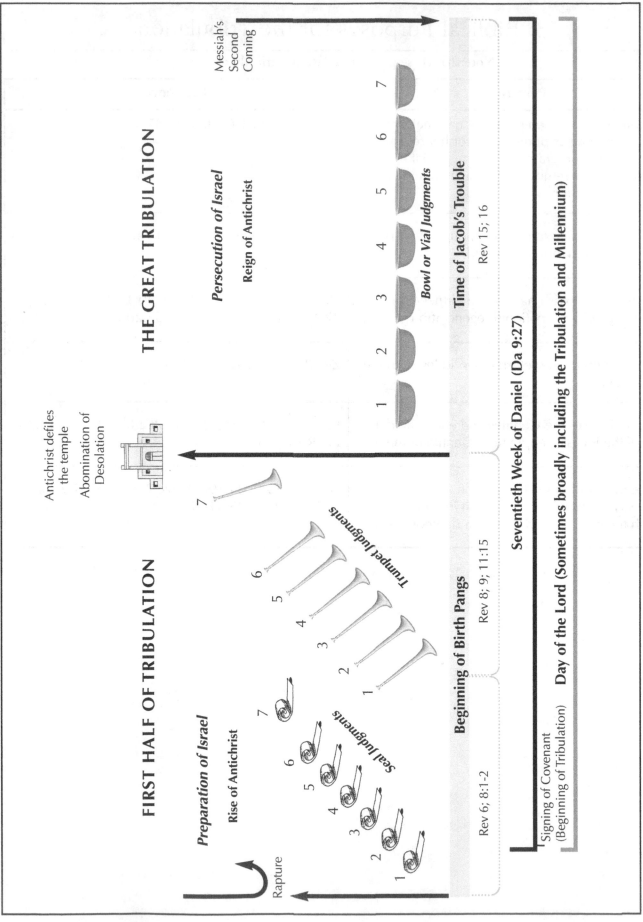

FIRST HALF OF TRIBULATION

Preparation of Israel

Rise of Antichrist

Rapture

Seal Judgments

7 6 5 4 3 2 1

Trumpet Judgments

7 6 5 4 3 2 1

Antichrist defiles the temple
Abomination of Desolation

THE GREAT TRIBULATION

Persecution of Israel

Reign of Antichrist

Messiah's Second Coming

Bowl or Vial Judgments

1 2 3 4 5 6 7

Beginning of Birth Pangs

Rev 6; 8:1-2   Rev 8; 9; 11:15

Time of Jacob's Trouble

Rev 15; 16

Seventieth Week of Daniel (Da 9:27)

Signing of Covenant (Beginning of Tribulation)

Day of the Lord (Sometimes broadly including the Tribulation and Millennium)

75. New Testament Tribulation Terms and Expressions

Tribulation Term	New Testament Reference
The day	1Th 5:4
Those days	Mt 24:22; Mk 13:20
The Day of the Lord	1Th 5:2
The wrath	1Th 5:9; Rev 11:18
The wrath to come	1Th 1:10
The great day of their wrath	Rev 6:17
The wrath of God	Rev 15:1, 7; 14:10, 19; 16:1
The wrath of the Lamb	Rev 6:16
The hour of trial	Rev 3:10
The Tribulation	Mt 24:29; Mk 13:24
[Time of] tribulation	Mk 13:19
The Great Tribulation	Mt 24:21; Rev 2:22; 7:14
The hour of judgment	Rev 14:7
Birth pangs	Mt 24:8

76. Old Testament Tribulation Terms and Expressions

Tribulation Term	Old Testament Reference
Birth pangs	Isa 21:3; 26:17-18; 66:7; Jer 4:31; Mic 4:10 (cf. Jer 30:6)
Day of the Lord	Ob 15; Joel 1:15; 2:1, 11, 31; 3:14; Am 5:18, 20; Isa 2:12; 13:6, 9; Zep 1:7, 14; Eze 13:5; 30:3; Zec 14:1
Great and terrible day of the Lord (LXX)	Mal 4:5
Day of wrath	Zep 1:15
Day of the Lord's wrath	Zep 1:18
Day of distress	Zep 1:15
Day of trouble	Zep 1:15
Day of desolation	Zep 1:15
Day of vengeance	Isa 34:8; 35:4; 61:2; 63:4
Day of Jacob's trouble	Jer 30:7
Day of darkness and gloominess	Zep 1:15; Am 5:18, 20; Joel 2:2
Day of clouds and thick darkness	Zep 1:15; Joel 2:2
Day of trumpet and battle cry	Zep 1:16
Day of alarm	Zep 1:16
Day of the Lord's anger	Zep 2:2-3
[Day of] destruction, ruin from the Almighty	Joel 1:15
Day of calamity, distress	Dt 32:35; Ob 12-14
Trouble, tribulation	Dt 4:30; Zep 1:16
One week (Daniel's Seventieth Week)	Da 9:27
Time/day of trouble, distress	Da 12:1; Zep 1:15
The indignation	Isa 26:20
The overflowing scourge	Isa 28:15, 18
The fire of His jealousy	Zep 1:18

Unless otherwise noted, the NKJV is used in this chart.

77. Contrasts between Christ and the Antichrist

Christ	Antichrist
Image of God (Jn 14:9)	Image of Satan (Rev 12:3; 13:1; 17:3)
Descended from above (Jn 6:38)	Ascends from the pit (Rev 11:7)
Holy One [of God] (Mk 1:24)	Lawless one (2Th 2:8)
Son of God (Lk 1:35)	Son of perdition (2Th 2:3)
Came in Father's name (Jn 5:43a)	Comes in own name (Jn 5:43b)
Came to do Father's will (Jn 6:38)	Comes to do his own will (Da 11:36)
Second person of the Holy Trinity (Father, Son, Holy Spirit)	Second person of Unholy Trinity (Satan, Antichrist, False Prophet)
Mystery of godliness (1Ti 3:16)	Mystery of iniquity (2Th 2:7)
Man of sorrows (Isa 53:3)	Man of sin (2Th 2:3)
He is the truth (Jn 14:6)	He is a liar (2Th 2:9-10)
Humbled himself (Php 2:6-8)	Exalts himself (2Th 2:4)
Came as a Savior (Lk 19:10)	Comes as a destroyer (Da 8:24)
Cleansed the temple (Jn 2:14-17)	Desecrates the temple (2Th 2:4)
Despised and rejected (Isa 53:3; Lk 23:18)	Desired and revered (Rev 13:3-4)
The Good Shepherd (Jn 10:1-15)	The evil (worthless) shepherd (Zec 11:16)
Exalted by God to heaven (Php 2:9-11)	Cast down by God to hell (Rev 19:20)
His bride, the church, will be glorified (Eph 5:25-27)	His harlot, the apostate church, will be burned (Rev 17:1-16)
Possesses deity (Jn 20:28; Rev 1:8, 17)	Professes deity (Da 11:36; 2Th 2:4)
The King of Kings (Rev. 1:5; 15:3; 17:14; 19:16)	A king of the earth (Da 7:8, 24; Rev 13:7

Chart 77—*Contrasts between Christ and the Antichrist (Cont.)*

Christ	Antichrist
Has seven horns (kingdoms); perfect rule (Rev 5:6)	Has ten horns (kingdoms); limited rule (Rev 13:1; 17:12)
Speech submissive to Father's will (Jn 14:10)	Blasphemous speech (Rev 13:5-6)
Meek and lowly (Mt 11:29)	Arrogant and self-willed (Da 7:25)
"Faithful and True" (Rev 3:14; 19:11)	Master of deceit (Da 8:23)
Shepherds the saints (Rev 7:15-17)	Makes war with the saints (Da 7:21)
Brings peace on earth (Zec 9:10; Ro 16:20; Eph 2:14)	Takes peace from the earth (Rev 6:4)
Smites the nations (Ps 2:9; Rev 19:5)	
Fulfills covenant with Israel (Eze 37:26; Ro 11:27)	
Builds temple (Zec 6:12-13)	Blasphemy in temple (2Th 2:4)
Speaks words of life (Jn 6:23)	Speaks words of death (Rev 13:15)
Controlled by Holy Spirit (Lk 4:1)	Controlled by demonic spirits (Rev 16:13-14)
Comes to save Israel (Zec 12:10-13:5; Mt 24:30-31)	Comes to destroy Israel (Rev 12:1-6, 13-17)
Comes with a sword (Rev 19:15)	Comes with a bow (Rev 6:2)
Reigns in New Jerusalem (Rev 21:22-27)	Desecrates earthly Jerusalem (Rev 11:2)
Destiny is at right hand of God (Mt 26:64; Ac 7:56)	Destiny is lake of fire (Rev 19:20)

78. Abomination of Desolation

First Half of Seventieth Week	Second Half of Seventieth Week
1. Preliminary tribulation (Mt 24:9-13; Mk 13:9-13)	1. Great Tribulation (Mt 24:16-22; Mk 13:15-20)
2. Signs on earth (Mt 24:6-8; Mk 13:7-8)	2. False messiahs (Mt 24:23-28; Mk 13:21-23)
3. False messiahs (Mt 24:5; Mk 13:5-6)	3. Signs in heaven (Mt 24:29; Mk 13:24-25)
4. Prediction of destruction of temple and Jerusalem (Mt 23:37-24:2; Mk 13:2)	4. Final destruction at the eschaton (Mt 24:30-33; Mk 13:26-27)
Desecration series	Restoration series

79. Identity of the Antichrist through the Centuries

Antichrist is:	Held by:
1. Docetism or Gnosticism	Polycarp
2. Rome, the fourth empire of the vision of Daniel	Barnabas
3. Nero, to be raised from the dead	Victorinus
4. Roman Catholic Church and the papacy	Martin Luther and John Calvin
5. Luther and the Protestant churches	Roman Catholic writers
6. Napoléon	Various writers of that time
7. Nero, All details of the Revelation refer to the first century A.D. "The Lord revealed from heaven" refers to the destruction of Jerusalem. The first resurrection also occurs at the destruction of Jerusalem.	Milton Terry, *On Hermeneutics*
8. The beast out of the sea (Rev 13:1-8) is the Roman Empire (Diocletian), and the beast out of the earth is the Papacy.	E. W. Hengstenberg, Philip Mauro
9. The beast out of the earth (Rev 13:11-18) is the Roman hierarchy during the time of the Spanish Inquisition (16th century); fire from heaven is the Inquisition itself.	Adam Clark, Patrick Fairbairn
10. An embodiment of Satan	R. C. Trench
11. The "lawless one" in 2Th is a Jewish false Christ held in check by the Roman Empire. The first beast (Rev 13:1-8) is the restored Roman Empire; the second beast (Rev 13:11-18) is pseudo-prophecy supporting the first beast.	Bernard Weiss
12. An openly infidel supplanter of papacy	A. R. Fausset
13. Last ecclesiastical head, an apostate from Christianity (the beast out of the earth)	C. I. Scofield
14. Last ecclesiastical head, an apostate Jew (the beast out of the earth)	H. A. Ironside, Arno C. Gaebelein
15. The first beast is the Antichrist; the second beast is the False Prophet who supports him.	J. N. Darby, W. R. Newell, also J. Seiss, J. Dwight Pentecost, Donald Grey Barnhouse, Hal Lindsey, W. A. Criswell. These men also believe that it may be Judas Iscariot resurrected.

80. The Battle of Armageddon

The Reason for Armageddon

The reason for the battle of Armageddon may be said to be judgment upon the nations:

1. Because they have scattered Israel and appropriated Israel's land (Joel 3:2)

2. Because of their wickedness (Rev 16:14; 19:15)

3. Because of their failure to glorify God (Rev 16:9)

The Time of Armageddon

The battle of Armageddon will take place at the very end of the tribulation period. The time is further specified as:

1. The pouring out of the sixth bowl of God's wrath (Rev 16:12)

2. The second coming of Christ (Rev 11:16; Zec 14:4; Joel 3:15-16)

3. The time of Israel's regathering (Joel 3:1; Zep 3:20)

The Result of Armageddon

The battle of Armageddon will result in an ultimate victory for Christ (Rev 19:11-21). The armies of the earth will be defeated by the Lord at his second coming. The Beast and the False Prophet will be cast into a lake of fire. Satan will be bound and the armies of the earth slain and eaten by birds and vultures. The instrumental means used by Christ to destroy the Antichrist and the armies of the earth at his return are described poetically as:

1. A plague, causing tumult and mutiny (Zec 14:2-3)

2. Superhuman strength given to the believing remnant (Zec 12:6)

3. The brightness of his coming (2 Th 2:8-9)

Raymond Ludwigson, *A Survey of Bible Prophecy* (Grand Rapids: Zondervan, 1973), 19-20.

81. Proposed Times for the Battle of Gog and Magog (Eze 38–39)

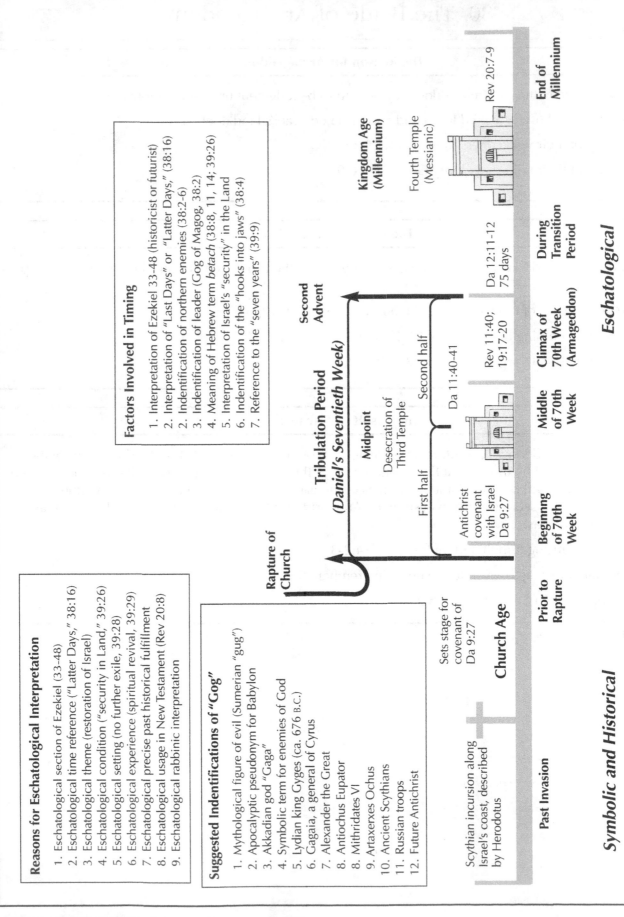

Reasons for Eschatological Interpretation

1. Eschatological section of Ezekiel (33–48)
2. Eschatological time reference ("Latter Days," 38:16)
3. Eschatological theme (restoration of Israel)
4. Eschatological condition ("security in Land," 39:26)
5. Eschatological setting (no further exile, 39:28)
6. Eschatological experience (spiritual revival, 39:29)
7. Eschatological precise past historical fulfillment
8. Eschatological usage in New Testament (Rev 20:8)
9. Eschatological rabbinic interpretation

Suggested Indentifications of "Gog"

1. Mythological figure of evil (Sumerian "gug")
2. Apocalyptic pseudonym for Babylon
3. Akkadian god "Gaga"
4. Symbolic term for enemies of God
5. Lydian king Gyges (ca. 676 B.C.)
6. Gagaia, a general of Cyrus
7. Alexander the Great
8. Antiochus Eupator
8. Mithridates VI
9. Artaxerxes Ochus
10. Ancient Scythians
11. Russian troops
12. Future Antichrist

Factors Involved in Timing

1. Interpretation of Ezekiel 33–48 (historicist or futurist)
2. Interpretation of "Last Days" or "Latter Days," (38:16)
2. Indentification of northern enemies (38:2-6)
3. Indentification of leader (Gog of Magog, 38:2)
4. Meaning of Hebrew term *betach* (38:8, 11, 14; 39:26)
5. Interpretation of Israel's "security" in the Land
6. Indentification of the "hooks into jaws" (38:4)
7. Reference to the "seven years" (39:9)

Rapture of Church

Second Advent

Tribulation Period (Daniel's Seventieth Week)

Midpoint — Desecration of Third Temple

First half · Second half

Antichrist covenant with Israel Da 9:27

Da 11:40-41

Rev 11:40; 19:17-20

Da 12:11-12 75 days

Rev 20:7-9

Kingdom Age (Millennium)

Fourth Temple (Messianic)

Sets stage for covenant of Da 9:27

Scythian incursion along Israel's coast, described by Herodotus

| Past Invasion | Church Age | Prior to Rapture | Beginning of 70th Week | Middle of 70th Week | Climax of 70th Week (Armageddon) | During Transition Period | End of Millennium |

Symbolic and Historical   *Eschatological*

82. A Biblical Case for Divine Causation (Basis for Prophetic Judgment)

Sinful Incident	Responsible Agent	Sovereign Cause	Purpose/Result
Selling of Joseph into slavery	Brothers (Ge 37:26-28)	God (Ge 45:8)	Salvation (preservation of Israelites) (Ge 50:20)
Obdurate resistance to God's command (Ex 4:21; Ge 15:13-14)	Pharaoh (Ex 8:15)	God (Ex 4:21)	Salvation (deliverance) of Israel and demonstration of power of God (Ex 3:19-20; 9:16)
Rejection of request for Israelite passage	Sihon (Nu 21:23)	God (Dt 2:30)	Provision of land for Israel (Dt 2:31)
Failure of Israelites to understand and believe God	Sons of Israel (Ps 106:7)	God (Dt 29:4)	Example for instruction of elect in holiness (1Co 10:6, 11)
Opposition to Israelite settlement in Canaan (cf. Ge 15:16)	Kings of Canaan (Jos 11:18-19; cf. Ps 105:25)	God (Jos 11:20)	Retributive judgment on degenerate paganism; conquest and settlement of Canaan (Jos 11:20)
Defeat of Israel in battle (Dt 28:25)	Enemies of Israel (e.g., Jdg 3:8)	God (Jdg 3:8, 12; 4:2; 6:1; 10:7; 13:1)	Discipline of Israel, leading to repentance and to establishment of new Judge/Deliverer (Jdg 3:9-10)
Destruction of Shechem Death of Abimelech	Evil spirit, citizens of Shechem, woman, armor bearer (Jdg 9:23-25, 53-54)	God (Jdg 9:23, 56)	Execution of justice (defense of the innocent and punishment of the violent) (Jdg 9:42, 57)
Failure to repent of disobedience	Sons of Eli (1Sa 2:25a)	God (1Sa 2:25b)	Provision of priesthood and judgeship to Samuel (1Sa 3:13; 5:11)
Murderous intent (1Sa 15:26)	Evil spirit, Saul (1Sa 18:10; 19:9-10; 20:30-33)	God (1Sa 16:14-16, 23)	To lead Saul to judgment and to prepare David for rule (1Sa 15:28)
Suicide of Saul (1Sa 28:19)	Saul (1Ch 10:4)	God (1Ch 10:14)	Discipline/judgment on Saul; establishment of David (1Ch 10:14)
Death of David's infant (2Sa 12:14b)	Sickness (2Sa 12:15b)	God (2Sa 12:15a)	Restoration of God's reputation in Israel (2Sa 12:14a)
Absalom's defilement (2Sa 12:11)	Absalom (and Ahithophel) (2Sa 16:20-23)	God (2Sa 12:12)	Discipline of David and restoration of divine reputation defiled by David (cf. 2Sa 12:14)
Deception of Hushai	Hushai (2Sa 17:7-13)	God (2Sa 17:14a)	To thwart Absalom's usurption of David (2Sa 17:14b; 18:31)

Chart 82—*A Biblical Case for Divine Causation (Cont.)*

Sinful Incident	Responsible Agent	Sovereign Cause	Purpose/Result
Cursing of David	Shimei (2Sa 16:5-9)	God (2Sa 16:10-11)	Discipline of David (result: blessing of David) (2Sa 16:12)
Sinful census	Satan (and David) (1Ch 21:1; 2Sa 24:1)	God (2Sa 24:17; 24:1, 18)	Discipline of Israel (result: site of temple)
Followed foolish counsel (1Ki 11:29-36)	Rehoboam (2Ch 10:13-15)	God (2Ch 10:15)	Confirmation of prophetic program (2Ch 10:15)
Deception and death of Ahab (1Ki 21:19)	Deceptive spirit	God (1Ki 22:22-23)	Removal of faithless king (1Ki 21:22, 25)
Disbelief and disobedience (Isa 6:9-10)	Judeans (Isa 6:10; 29:13; cf. Ac 28:27)	God (Isa 6:9)	Removal of faithless to allow for remnant of the faithful; inclusion of Gentile elect (Isa 6:13; Ro 11:7-11; cf. Eze 36:16-38; 37:1-14; Isa 9:1-2)
Ruination of many nations (Isa 15:5-23:18, etc.)	Enemy nations (e.g., Egypt, Assyria, Babylon)	God (Isa 10:5; 13:3, 17, 19:2, 14; cf. 40:15-17, 23-24)	Demonstration of God's sovereign rule, both to nations and to his elect (cf. Isa 19:22-25; 41:1-4; Eze 36:22-24)
Ministry of hardening	Rejection by Judas	Rejection by Gentiles	Rejection by Jews

Ministry of Messiah		Rejection of Messiah	
Mt 13:10-15	Mt 26:24; Lk 22:22	Ac 4:25-28	Jn 10-26; 12:37-40
Mk 4:11-12	Jn 6:64-65; 13:18-19	2Th 2:11-12	Ac 4:27-28; 28:24-28
Lk 8:10	Ac 1:16-20	Rev 13:8; 17:8, 17	Ro 9:10-23; 11:7-10
			1Pe 2:8 (cf. Pr 16:4)

PART 9

The Olivet Discourse

83. The Olivet Discourse

PARALLELS BETWEEN MATTHEW AND REVELATION		
	Matthew	**Revelation**
First Half of Tribulation		
Antichrist	24:5	6:2
Wars, terror	24:6-7	6:3-4
Famines	24:7	6:5-6
Pestilence, earthquakes	24:7-8	6:7-8
Saints killed	24:9	6:9-11
Second Half of Tribulation		
Antichrist's persecutions	24:9	12:12-17
Many are deceived	24:10-12	13:11-18
Many will believe	24:13-14	7:1-17
Antichrist in temple	24:15	13:4-5
Israel to flee	24:16-20	12:12-17
Tribulation's length	24:21-22	11:3; 12:6, 14; 13:5
Signs and wonders	24:23-26	13:13-14
Second Coming of Christ		
Preparations	24:27-28	19:1-8
Supernatural signs	24:29	16:8-11
Battle of Armageddon	24:30	19:19
Visible to all	24:30	19:11-16
Regathering of Israel	24:31	(Ro 9:11)
Practical Challenges		
Various parables	24:32-25:30	2:10, 25; 3:3, 10-12, 21
Judgment of Gentiles	25:31-46	11:18; 19:15; 14:19

84. Futurist Interpretation of the Olivet Discourse

(Based on the Desecration and Restoration of the Temple as an Eschatological Motif)

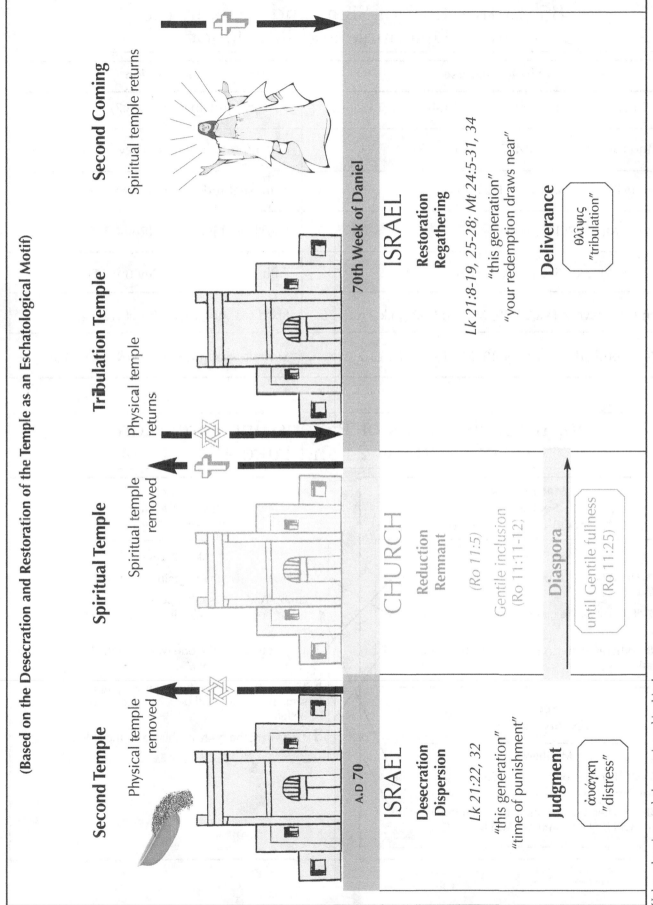

Second Temple

Physical temple removed

A.D 70

ISRAEL

Desecration
Dispersion

Lk 21:22, 32

"this generation"
"time of punishment"

Judgment

ἀνάγκη
"distress"

Spiritual Temple

Spiritual temple removed

CHURCH

Reduction
Remnant

(Ro 11:5)

Gentile inclusion
(Ro 11:11-12)

Diaspora

until Gentile fullness
(Ro 11:25)

Tribulation Temple

Physical temple returns

70th Week of Daniel

ISRAEL

Restoration
Regathering

Lk 21:8-19, 25-28; Mt 24:5-31, 34

"this generation"
"your redemption draws near"

Deliverance

θλῖψις
"tribulation"

Second Coming

Spiritual temple returns

Unless otherwise noted, the NKJV is used in this chart.

85. Correlation of Signs and Seals in the Olivet Discourse and Revelation

Olivet Discourse	Revelation
False Christs and False Prophets (Mt 24:4-5; Mk 13:21-22)	First seal judgment (Rev 6:2)
Wars and rumors of war (Mt 24:6; Mk 13:7)	Second seal judgment (Rev 6:3-4)
Famines (Mt 24:7; Mk 13:8; Lk 21:11)	Third seal judgment (Rev 6:5-6)
Pestilence (Mt 24:7; Lk 21:11)	Fourth seal judgment (Rev 6:7-8)
Tribulation (Mt 24:15, 21; Mk 13:19)	Fifth seal judgment (Rev 6:9-11)
Signs in the heavens (Mt 24:29; Mk 13:24-25; Lk 21:25-26)	Sixth seal judgment (Rev 6:12-14)
Christ's second advent (Mt 24:30; Mk 13:26; Lk 21:27)	Seventh seal judgment (Rev 19:11-16)

86. Inconsistencies of Preterist Interpretation of Matthew 24 and Luke 17

Matthew 24
Section A
(Events Relating to A.D. 70)

Matthew 24:1-34

1 17-18 "Whoever is on the housetop must not go down."

2 27 "For just as the lightning comes from the east …"

3 28 "Wherever the corpse is, there the vultures will gather."

Section B
(Events Still Future)

Matthew 24:35ff.

4 37-39 "For the coming of the Son of Man will be just like the days of Noah."

5 40-41 "Then there shall be two men in the field; one will be taken and one will be left."

Lk 17
All One Section
(Events Mixed)

Luke 17:20-37

2 24 "For just like the lightning, when it flashes …"

4 26-27 "And just as it happened in the days of Noah, so it will be also in the days of the Son of Man."

1 31 "On that day, the one who is on the housetop … must not go down."

5 35-36 "There will be two women grinding at the same place; one will be taken and the other will be left."

3 37 "Where the body is, there also the vultures will be gathered."

Chart compiled by Edward E. Stevens.
Scripture references from NASB.

PART 10

Teaching on the Millennium

87. Views on the Millennium

HISTORIC PREMILLENNIALISM
(Also called classical and nondispensational premillennialism)

Statement of View	Premillennialists hold that the return of Christ will be preceded by certain signs, then followed by a period of peace and righteousness in which Christ will reign on earth in person as King. Historic premillennialists understand the return of Christ and the Rapture as one and the same event. They see unity. Therefore they stand apart from the dispensational premillennialists, who see these as two events separated by the 7-year Tribulation. Premillennialism was the dominant eschatological interpretation in the first three centuries of the Christian church. Early fathers Papias, Irenaeus, Justin Martyr, Tertullian, and others held to this view.
Proponents	George E. Ladd, J. Barton Payne, Alexander Reese, Millard Erickson

Arguments For	Arguments Against
The chronology of Rev 10-20 shows that immediately following the second coming of Christ the following will occur: the binding of Satan (20:1-3), the first resurrection (20:4-6), and the beginning of the reign of Christ (20:4-7) for a "thousand years." (pp. 17-18)*	The reign of Christ does not begin after the first resurrection, for he now reigns at the right hand of the Father (Heb 1:3). (pp. 178-79)
At the present time, the church is the spiritual Israel. God will return the nation of Israel to her rightful place to fulfill the promises of the kingdom (Ro 11) in the millennial kingdom. This passage supports the teaching of v. 24: "How much more readily will these, who are the natural branches, be grafted into their own olive tree!" (pp. 18-29)	While the church benefits spiritually from the promises made to Israel, Israel and the church are never specifically equated. (pp. 42-44) A kingdom composed of both glorified saints and people still in the flesh seems too unreal to be possible. (p. 49)
Both the Old Testament and Christ predicted a kingdom in which the Anointed One would rule (Ps 2; Mt 25:24).	The kingdom is an overall teaching of the Bible. It now lies in the church (Mt 12:28; Lk 17:20-21). Christ now reigns in heaven (Heb 1:3; 2:7-8). (pp. 178-79)
As the prophecies of the Old Testament were fulfilled in the past, so those concerning the future will be, too. This is an argument for consistency in hermeneutics. (pp. 27-29)	The interpretation of Rev 20:1-7 does not necessitate literalism. These verses can be understood symbolically, since the book of Revelation employs many symbols. (p. 161)
The church serves to fulfill some of the promises made to Israel. Christ made this clear after the Jews rejected him (Mt 12:28; Lk 17:20-21). (pp. 20-26)	Historic premillennialism insists that the New Testament interprets the Old Testament prophecies in cases where the New Testament is actually applying a principle found in an Old Testament prophecy (Hos 11:1 in Mt 2:15; Hos 1:10 and 2:23 in Ro 9:24-26). (pp. 42-43)
Many of the early church fathers held to this view of eschatology. (p. 9)	It is not easy to definitely place the church fathers into one view of eschatology. Also, doctrine is not determined by a survey of church fathers, but by study of Scripture. (p. 41)

*Unless otherwise indicated, the page numbers following statements refer to pages in Robert G. Clouse, *The Meaning of the Millennium: Four Views* (Downers Grove, IL: InterVarsity Press, 1977). Other references are for Enns, *The Moody Handbook of Theology;* Erickson, *Christian Theology,* 2d ed.; Anthony Hoekema, *The Bible and the Future* (Grand Rapids: Wm. B. Eerdmans, 1986).

Chart 87—*Views on the Millennium (Cont.)*

A literal 1,000-year earthly reign is referred to in only one passage (Rev 20:1-6), and it is mentioned in apocalyptic literature. The Old Testament cannot be used to supply material on the Millennium. (p. 32)	The Old Testament prophecies provide the basis for New Testament prophecies. The New Testament sets the place and duration of the Millennium (Rev 20:1-6), and the Old Testament gives much of the nature of the Millennium. (pp. 43-46)
Ro 11:26 says that national Israel will be converted (pp. 27-28).	Many passages in the New Testament dissolve distinctions between Israel and the church (Gal 2:28-29; 3:7; Eph 2:14-16). (p. 109)
God has made a special place for national Israel in his program (27-28).	Israel was chosen as the nation through which the Messiah would come. Since Jesus finished his work, Israel's unique purpose has been fulfilled. (p. 53)

DISPENSATIONAL PREMILLENNIALISM

Statement of View	Adherents of this school generally hold to the concept of two stages in the coming of Christ. He will come for his church (Rapture) and then with his church (Revelation). The two events are separated by a 7-year Tribulation. There is a consistent distinction between Israel and the church throughout history.
Proponents	J. N. Darby, C. I. Scofield, Lewis Sperry Chafer, John Walvoord, Charles Feinberg, Herman Hoyt, Harry Ironside, Alva McClain, Eric Sauer, Charles Ryrie

Arguments For	Arguments Against
Dispensational premillennialism maintains a consistent hermeneutic that recognizes that both the promise given to Israel and the promises to the church are to be fulfilled. (pp. 66-68)	The promise of land to Israel was fulfilled in Jos 21:43,45. Its purpose of bringing forth the Messiah has also been fulfilled. (p. 101)
The "coming to life" (Rev 20:4-5) being designated as the first resurrection supports two stages in the return of Christ.	This resurrection of Rev 20:4-5 precedes the millennial reign. (pp. 37-38)
Scripture reveals both a universal and a mediatorial kingdom, which are two aspects of God's rule. The mediatorial kingdom is the Millennium, in which Christ will reign on earth. (pp. 72-73ff.; 91)	God's rule over the creation has always been through a mediator. Thus, his mediatorial rule cannot be restricted to the Millennium. (p. 93)
A literal reading of Rev 19-20 leads to a dispensational premillennial view. Other views must spiritualize the events.	Much of Revelation must be understood symbolically because of its apocalyptic nature.
The Abrahamic covenant will be completely fulfilled in Israel (Ge 12:1-3). Its outworking is seen in the Palestinian, Davidic, and new covenants. The church shares the blessings of the new covenant but does not fulfill its promises (Gal 3:16).	The promises made to Old Testament Israel were always conditional, based on Israel's obedience and faithfulness. The new covenant is for the church, not for Israel. (p. 100)
The concept of a literal earthly kingdom is an outgrowth of the overall kingdom teachings in both the Old and New Testaments. (pp. 42-43)	The New Testament, which is the sole authority for the church, replaced the Old Testament and its promises. (p. 97)
The Millennium is possible and necessary because not all of the promises given to Israel have been fulfilled. (Enns, p. 390)	Israel's disobedience negated their promises, which were based on their faithfulness (Jer 18:9-10). (p. 98)

Chart 87—*Views on the Millennium (Cont.)*

The Old Testament describes the kingdom as a literal earthly reign of Messiah over the whole world. (pp. 79-84)	The New Testament shows that Christ established a kingdom at his first coming and is now reigning over the whole world. (p. 102)

POSTMILLENNIALISM

Statement of View	Postmillennialists believe that the kingdom of God is now extended through teaching, preaching, evangelization, and missionary activities. The world is to be Christianized, and the result will be a long period of peace and prosperity called the Millennium. This will be followed by Christ's return. This position is seemingly gaining more adherents in contemporary circles, such as the Christian Reconstruction Institute for Christian Studies. The leading proponent of traditional post-millennium was Loraine Boettner. See his book *The Millennium* (Philadelphia: Presbyterian and Reformed Publishing, 1957).
Proponents	Augustine, Loraine Boettner, A. Hodge, Charles Hodge, W. G. T. Shedd, A. H. Strong, B. B. Warfield, Joachim of Fiore, Daniel Whitby, James Snowden, Christian Reconstructionists

Arguments For	Arguments Against
The rule of the Spirit of God in the heart of the believer is in one sense a millennium (Jn 14-16). (p. 121)	Postmillennialism fails to deal adequately with Rev 20 in formulating and defining its concept of the Millennium. (Erickson, p. 1208)
The universal diffusion of the gospel is promised by Christ (Mt 28:18-20).	The Great Commission does command universal gospel proclamation, but the world is characterized by spiritual decline, not spiritual growth.
Christ's throne is in heaven, where he is now reigning and ruling (Pss 47:2; 97:5). The church has the job of proclaiming that truth and seeing people come to faith in him. (pp. 118-19)	Neither of these statements necessitates postmillennialism or precludes a future earthly reign.
Salvation will come to all nations, tribes, peoples, and tongues (Rev 7:9-10).	While salvation will come to all nations, this does not mean that all, or nearly all, will be saved. Nor does the New Testament say that the gospel is designed to improve social conditions in the world.
Christ's parable of the mustard seed shows how the gospel will extend and expand, slowly but surely, until it covers the whole world (Mt 13:31-32). The saved will far outnumber the lost in the world. (pp. 150-51)	A majority of saved people on earth does not guarantee the golden age that postmillennialism expects to come.
Much evidence exists that shows that where the gospel is preached, social and moral conditions are greatly improved.	The attitude of idealistic optimism overlooks the passages that reveal the distress and apostasy of the end times (Mt 24:3-14; 1Ti 4:1-5; 2Ti 3:1-7). Also, just as much evidence can be gathered to prove that world conditions are declining. (p. 151)
Through the preaching of the gospel and the saving work of the Spirit, the world will be Christianized, and Christ will return at the end of a long period of peace, commonly called the Millennium. (p. 118)	The use of an allegorical approach to the interpretation of Rev 20 is completely allegorizing the 1,000-year reign. There is a limited amount of scriptural support for postmillenialism.

Chart 87—*Views on the Millennium (Cont.)*

AMILLENNIALISM

Statement of View	The Bible predicts a continuous, parallel growth of good and evil in the world between the first and second comings of Christ. The kingdom of God is now present in the world through his Word, his Spirit, and his church. This position has also been called "realized millennialism."
Proponents	Oswald Allis, Louis Berkhof, G. Berkouwer, William Hendriksen, Abraham Kuyper, Leon Morris, Anthony Hoekema, other Reformed theologians, and the Roman Catholic Church.

Arguments For	Arguments Against
The conditional nature of the Abrahamic covenant (as well as the other covenants) indicates that fulfillment, or the lack of it, is transferred to the church through Jesus Christ (Ge 12:1-3; Ro 10; Gal 3:16).	Many passages show that the Abrahamic covenant was unconditional and was to be literally fulfilled by Israel.
The land promises of the Abrahamic covenant were expanded from the Jews to all believers, and from the land of Canaan to the new earth.	Amillennialism has problems in being hermeneutically consistent in the interpretation of the Scriptures. It spiritualizes passages that can clearly be understood literally.
Prophecy demands a symbolic approach to interpreting the Bible. Therefore, prophetic passages can be understood in the overall framework of God's outworking of the new covenant (e.g., Rev. 20). (p. 161)	The chronology of Rev 19-20 is continuous and describes events that will occur in the end of the Tribulation and prior to the 1,000-year reign of Christ.
The Old and New Testaments are bound together in unity under the covenant of grace. Israel and the church are not two distinct programs but one unified outworking of God's purposes and plans. (p. 186)	Scripture does not clearly reveal a covenant of grace. This is a theological term coined to fit into the amillennial scheme of eschatology.
The kingdom of God is central in biblical history. It was central in the Old Testament, in Jesus' ministry, and in the church and will be consummated with Christ's return. There is no need to call for a kingdom at a latter time, for the kingdom has always been. (pp. 177-79)	The position clearly does not see God's having a place for Israel in the future. Amillennialists have difficulty explaining Ro 11.
History is moving toward the goal of the total redemption of the universe (Eph 1:10; Col 1:18). (p. 187)	The total redemption of the universe is the goal of all millennial views. This does not specifically support an amillennial view.
Rev 20:4-6 refers to the reign of souls with Christ in heaven as he reigns by his word and by his spirit. (pp. 164-66)	Rev 20:4-5 clearly refers to a resurrection, yet the amillennialists avoid the issue. Forms of the Greek word *zaō* (ζάω), "to live," are used in the same way for resurrection in Jn 5:25 and Rev 2:8.
The New Testament often equates Israel and the church; they are a unity (Ac 13:32-39; Gal 6:15; 1Pe 2:9). (Hoekema, 197-98)	National Israel and the church are treated as distinct in the New Testament (Ac 3:12; 4:8-10; 21:28; Ro 9:3-4; 10:1; 11; Eph 2:12).

88. Characteristics of the Millennium

Geographical	Social	Spiritual	Environmental
Increase in territory (Ge 15:18; Isa 26:15; Ob 1:17-21)	Universal knowledge of Lord (Isa 11:9; 54:13; Hab 2:14)	Universal worship (Isa 19:21; 52:1, 7-10; Mal 1:11; Zec 8:23)	Conditions of holiness (Isa 1:26-27; 35:8-10; Zep 3:11)
Topographical changes (Eze 47:8-12; Isa 2:2; Zec 14:4, 8, 10)	Reproduction by saints (Isa 65:23; Eze 47:21-22; Zec 10:8)	Rebuilt temple (Eze 37:26-28; Eze 40-48; Hag 2:7-9; Joel 3:18)	Restoration of Edenic conditions (Isa 11:6-9; 65:25)
Jerusalem as center of world's worship (Isa 2:2-3; Mic 4:1-2; Zec 8:3; 14:16-21)	Unimpaired labor (Eze 48:18-19; Isa 62:8-9; 65:21-23)	Return of the Shekinah glory (Eze 43:1-7; 48:35; Zec 2:10-13; Jer 3:17)	Removal of harmful effects (Isa 33:24; 35:5-7; Zep 3:19)
Enlargement of Jerusalem (Eze 48:35; Jer 3:17)	Universal language (Zep 3:9)	Revival of sacrificial system (Eze 43:13-27; 45:13-25; Isa 56:7)	Restoration of longevity (Isa 65:20)
Name of Jerusalem changed (Isa 62:2-4)	Freedom from war/enemies (Isa 2:4; 14:3-7; Zec 9:8; 14:10-11; Am 9:15)	Restoration of Sabbath and ritual feasts (Eze 44:24; Zec 14:16)	Increase in daylight (Isa 4:5-6; 30:26; 60:19-20; Zec 2:5)
Jews return and live in Land (Eze 36:24; 37:25)	Peaceful society (Isa 11:6-9; 65:21; Hos 2:18; Zec 9:10)	Spiritual obedience under new covenant (Eze 36:25-28; 37; Jer 31:31-34)	Economic prosperity (Isa 30:23-25; 35:1-7; Am 9:13-15; Joel 2:21-27)
Reversal of Land's desolate condition (Eze 36:33-36; 62:4)	Justice (Isa 9:6-7; 32:16; Jer 30:9; Eze 34:23; Hos 3:5)	Satan/demons bound; no spiritual deception (Rev 20:1-3)	Universal access to Israel (Isa 2:2-3; 11:16; 56:6; Jer 3:14-15)

89. Premillennial Interpretation of "Signs"

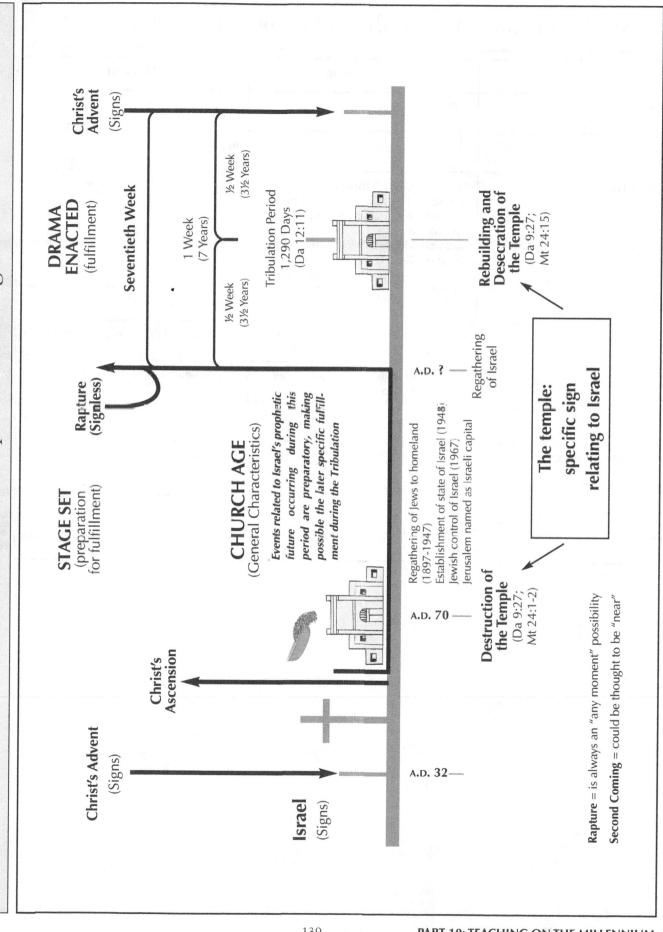

STAGE SET
(preparation for fulfillment)

Christ's Advent
(Signs)

Christ's Ascension

CHURCH AGE
(General Characteristics)

Events related to Israel's prophetic future occurring during this period are preparatory, making possible the later specific fulfillment during the Tribulation

Israel
(Signs)

A.D. 32—

A.D. 70 —

Destruction of the Temple
(Da 9:27; Mt 24:1-2)

Regathering of Jews to homeland (1897-1947)
Establishment of state of Israel (1948);
Jewish control of Israel (1967);
Jerusalem named as Israeli capital

A.D. ?

Regathering of Israel

Rapture
(Signless)

DRAMA ENACTED
(fulfillment)

Seventieth Week

½ Week (3½ Years)

1 Week (7 Years)

½ Week (3½ Years)

Tribulation Period 1,290 Days (Da 12:11)

Christ's Advent
(Signs)

Rebuilding and Desecration of the Temple
(Da 9:27; Mt 24:15)

The temple: specific sign relating to Israel

Rapture = is always an "any moment" possibility

Second Coming = could be thought to be "near"

PART 10: TEACHING ON THE MILLENNIUM

90. Contrasts between the Millennium and Heaven

	Millennium	Heaven
Duration	1,000 years (Rev 20:1-6)	Eternal (Rev 22:5)
Death	Possible (Isa 65:20)	Impossible (Rev 21:4)
Longevity of Life	"Never again will there be in [Jerusalem] an infant who lives but a few days, or an old man who does not live out his years; he who dies at a hundred will be thought a mere youth; he who fails to reach a hundred will be considered accursed." (Isa 65:20)	No aging (Rev 21:4, implied)
Sin Nature	Active (Rev 20:7-9)	Abolished (Rev 21:27)
Inhabitants	Initially believers only; later includes unbelievers (Mt 25:34; Rev 20:7-9)	Believers and God's angels (Rev 21:27)
Bodies	Mortal and immortal living together (Isa 62:20; 1Co 15:42-44)	Only immortal (glorified) (1Co 15:42-44)
Satan	Bound, but released after 1,000 years (Rev 20:3, 7)	In lake of burning sulfur, never to be released again (Rev 20:10)
Political and Religious Center	Jerusalem (Isa 2:2-3; Mic 4:1-2, 7)	New Jerusalem (Rev 21)
Place	Earth (Rev 5:10)	New heavens and new earth (Rev 21:1)
Key Passages	Ps 72; Isa 2; 11; 65-66; Rev 20:1-6	Rev 21-22

Adapted from Griffith, *Eschatology.*

PART 11

Daniel and Revelation

91. Evaluating Views on Daniel 9:24-27

| | HISTORICAL | | FUTURISTIC | |
	CRITICAL	MESSIANIC	SYMBOLIC	PREMILLENNIAL
Whose decree begins the seventy "sevens" (v 25)?	Jeremiah (Jer 25:11), referring to 605 B.C. or 586 B.C. (better)	Cyrus (538 B.C.) or Artaxerxes' 1st decree (457 B.C., Ezra)	Cyrus (538 B.C.)	Artaxerxes' 2d decree (444 B.C., Nehemiah)
When do the seventy "sevens" end (v. 27)?	Temple rededication (164 b.c.)	Stephen's death and Paul's call (A.D. 33)	Rapture of the church (no 7 yr. Tribulation)	Christ's return after the Tribulation
Who is the "Anointed One" and when does he "come" (vv. 25-27)?	Cyrus (538 B.C.) in v. 25 but Joshua the High Priest (457 B.C.) in v. 26	Christ at his Baptism (A.D. 26)	Christ at his Baptism (A.D. 26)	Christ at his Triumphal Entry (A.D. 33)
Who destroys the city and the temple (v. 26)?	Antiochus Epiphanes desecrates the temple	Titus destroys Jerusalem and the temple (A.D. 70)	Antichrist destroys the visible church	Titus destroys Jerusalem and the temple (A.D. 70)
Is there a gap between the 69th and the 70th "seven"?	No	No	No	Yes
Who makes covenant, ends sacrifice (v. 27)?	Antiochus Epiphanes (170-164 b.c.)	Christ (a.d. 26-33)	Antichrist	Antichrist (as antitype of Titus)
What's the covenant?	(Noncommittal view)	New Covenant	Covenant of terror	Peace with Jews
With whom is the covenant confirmed (who are the "many")?	Jerusalem Jews tired of Hellenistic (Greek) rule	Disciples at the Last Supper (extended to the church)	The Gentile masses who follow the Antichrist	End-time Jews (who are "[Daniel's] people," v. 24)
What is "the end to sacrifice" (v. 27)?	Offering a pig on the temple altar	Christ's death	Antichrist overthrows church's worship	Antichrist stops future Tribulation sacrifices
Who causes the desolations (v. 27b)? How?	Antiochus sets up a pagan emblem on the temple porch	Titus destroys Jerusalem and the temple (A.D. 70)	Antichrist's idols—materialism, goals, paradise without God, etc.	Antichrist insists that the Jews worship his image (Rev 13:14-15)
Problems	• Says prophecy is a forgery after the fact • Inconsistent identity of the Anointed One (vv. 25, 26) • Antiochus made no covenant with Jews • Antiochus did not destroy the city or temple (desecrated it only) and Jesus saw this as future (Mt 24:15; Mk 13:14)	• Inconsistent use of the word "seven" (in 538 b.c. reckoning) • Christ didn't make a covenant in a.d. 26 • Christ's death didn't end sacrifices—they continued to a.d. 70 • See "abomination" as a.d. 70 but before "week" of a.d. 26-33 • A seven-year period re: Christ does not exist	• Why all the specific "sevens" if earth is indefinite—not years? • "City and sanctuary" are allegorized to be the church • Daniel's people (Israel) is addressed, not the church masses • Stretches it to call "sacrifice and offering" the church's worship	Support: • The decree of 444 b.c. is the best date since it included both the city and walls (cf. Ne 2:3, 5, 8) • Employs 360-day (lunar) years of the Jewish calendar but still works with the Gregorian and even astronomical calendar • Deals fairly with a gap "after the sixty-two 'sevens'" (v. 26)

Chart 91—*Evaluating Views on Daniel 9:24-27 (Cont.)*

	• The city was *ruined* in 586, not *rebuilt* as required by v. 25 • 538 to 170 b.c. is only 369 years (not the required 62 x 7 = 434)—65 years off target • Accuses Daniel of mathematical errors	• Not 7 years between Christ's death and a.d. 70, so v. 27 not fulfilled literally • Rev 13:5, 14-15 (written a.d. 95) are future fulfillment • "He" (v. 27) looks back to Titus as antecedent (v. 26b), not to Christ (v. 26a)	• Overlapping of the sixty-two "sevens" and 70th "sevens" improbable • Francisco's teaching that Jerusalem has not yet been destroyed and that the present age is the last half-week denies history and allegorizes the text	• Allows a literal fulfillment of vv. 24, 27—neither of which is presently fulfilled • Considers v. 27 as future in line with Da 7:25; Rev 12, 13, 19
Advocates	Montgomery (ICC), Hartman & DiLella (AB), F. F. Bruce (but he notes future significance too)	E. J. Young, Pusey, J. Barton Payne	Leupold, Keil, McComisky, Francisco, *Review & Expositor* 57 (April 1960): 126-37	Hochner, Anderson, Walvoord, Whitcomb, Archer (but he says 457 b.c.-a.d. 27 for the sixty-nine "sevens")
Perspective	Liberal critical	Conservative amil or premil	Conservative amillennial	Conservative premillennial

†Due to varying opinions even within each of the four views, the chart mostly reflects opinions of their first advocate.

Griffith, *Escatology*; based on chart in J. Barton Payne, *The Theology of the Older Testament* (Grand Rapids: Zondervan, 1962), 250–52.

PART 11: DANIEL AND REVELATION

92. Historicist Chronology of the Seventy Weeks (Da 9:24-27)

Explanation of the historicist's Interpretation of Details of the Text

The "Messiah" (v. 25b) = "prince who is to come" (v. 26b) = price of the covenant (v. 27a) is the one whose own people (the Jewish Nation) "destroys the city [of Jerusalem] and the sanctuary" (v. 26c) by their rejection of His sacrificial work on the cross (A.D. 31). This judgment of desolation (v. 27d) was predicted (Mt 21:33-46; 23:37-39; Lk 23:28-31), but postponed in order to allow a day of grace and for the "abomination" (v. 27c) = Jewish rejection of their Messiah as depicted in the continuing sacrifical system, to reach its limit = "the wing" (v. 27c). Although sacrifice and offering did not actually cease at the midpoint of the 70th Week, it effectively ceased in that the ritual had lost its meaning with the death of Christ, and the city and Temple were no longer "holy" and were as good as destroyed since the cross sealed their doom and ultimately resulted in their physical destruction. The text does not give a time for the end of the 70th Week because it is not significant, however, this end was most likely with the stoning of Stephen, the first Christian martyr, which signaled the limit of Jewish rejection of Christ had been reached and terminated the allotted period of grace. With this understanding, every event falls within the 70 Weeks.

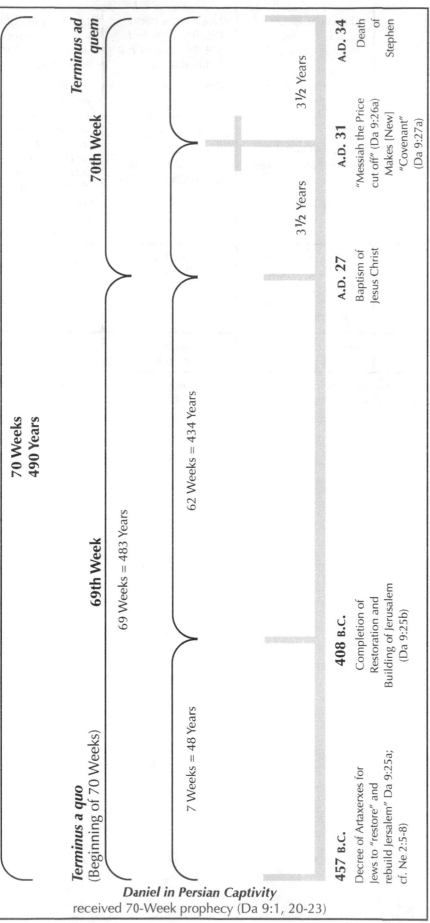

Terminus a quo
(Beginning of 70 Weeks)

Terminus ad quem

69th Week

70th Week

70 Weeks
490 Years

69 Weeks = 483 Years

62 Weeks = 434 Years

7 Weeks = 48 Years

3½ Years

3½ Years

457 B.C.
Decree of Artaxerxes for Jews to "restore" and rebuild Jersalem" Da 9:25a; cf. Ne 2:5-8)

408 B.C.
Completion of Restoration and Building of Jerusalem (Da 9:25b)

A.D. 27
Baptism of Jesus Christ

A.D. 31
"Messiah the Price cut off" (Da 9:26a) Makes [New] "Covenant" (Da 9:27a)

A.D. 34
Death of Stephen

Daniel in Persian Captivity
received 70-Week prophecy (Da 9:1, 20-23)

Scripture quotations are from NASB

Brempong Oswusu-Anti, *The Chronology of Daniel 9:24–27*. Adventist Theological Society Dissertation Series, vol. 2 (Berrien Springs, MI: Adventist Theological Society. 1995)

93. Futurist Chronology of the Seventy Weeks (Da 9:24-27)

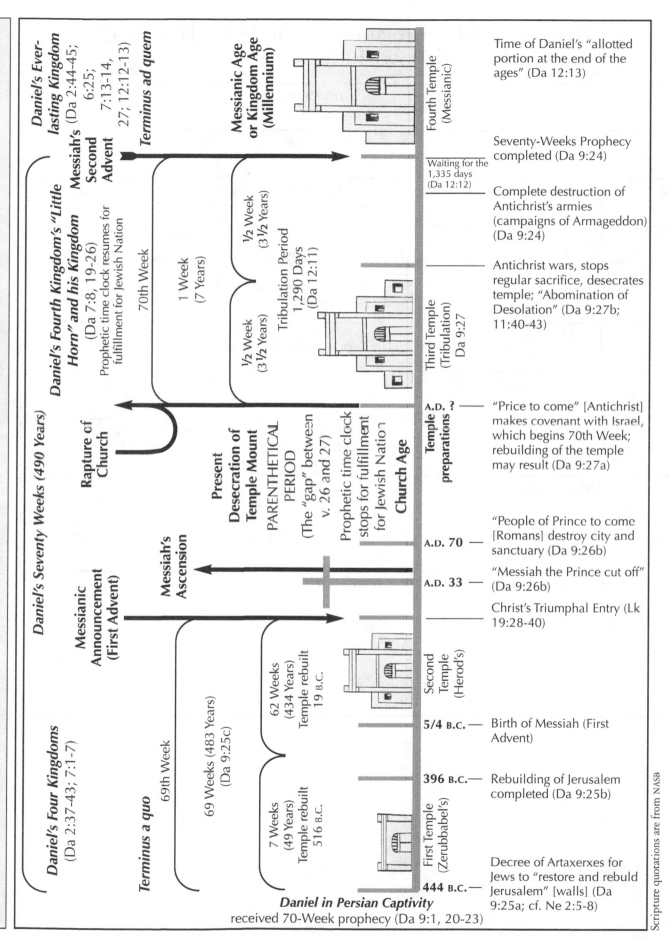

Time of Daniel's "allotted portion at the end of the ages" (Da 12:13)

Seventy-Weeks Prophecy completed (Da 9:24)

Complete destruction of Antichrist's armies (campaigns of Armageddon) (Da 9:24)

Antichrist wars, stops regular sacrifice, desecrates temple; "Abomination of Desolation" (Da 9:27b; 11:40-43)

"Price to come" [Antichrist] makes covenant with Israel, which begins 70th Week; rebuilding of the temple may result (Da 9:27a)

"People of Prince to come [Romans] destroy city and sanctuary (Da 9:26b)

"Messiah the Prince cut off" (Da 9:26b)

Christ's Triumphal Entry (Lk 19:28-40)

Birth of Messiah (First Advent)

Rebuilding of Jerusalem completed (Da 9:25b)

Decree of Artaxerxes for Jews to "restore and rebuild Jerusalem" [walls] (Da 9:25a; cf. Ne 2:5-8)

Daniel's Ever-lasting Kingdom (Da 2:44-45; 6:25; 7:13-14, 27; 12:12-13)

Terminus ad quem

Messiah's Second Advent

Daniel's Fourth Kingdom's "Little Horn" and his Kingdom (Da 7:8, 19-26)
Prophetic time clock resumes for fulfillment for Jewish Nation

Messianic Age or Kingdom Age (Millennium)

Fourth Temple (Messianic)

Waiting for the 1,335 days (Da 12:12)

70th Week

1 Week (7 Years)

½ Week (3½ Years)

Tribulation Period 1,290 Days (Da 12:11)

½ Week (3½ Years)

Third Temple (Tribulation) Da 9:27

A.D. ? Temple preparations

Daniel's Seventy Weeks (490 Years)

Rapture of Church

Present Desecration of Temple Mount
PARENTHETICAL PERIOD
(The "gap" between v. 26 and 27)
Prophetic time clock stops for fulfillment for Jewish Nation

Church Age

A.D. 70 —

Messiah's Ascension

A.D. 33 —

Messianic Announcement (First Advent)

Daniel's Four Kingdoms (Da 2:37-43; 7:1-7)

Terminus a quo

69th Week

69 Weeks (483 Years) (Da 9:25c)

62 Weeks (434 Years) Temple rebuilt 19 B.C.

7 Weeks (49 Years) Temple rebuilt 516 B.C.

Second Temple (Herod's)

5/4 B.C. —

396 B.C. —

First Temple (Zerubbabel's)

444 B.C. —

Daniel in Persian Captivity
received 70-Week prophecy (Da 9:1, 20-23)

Scripture quotations are from NASB

PART 11: DANIEL AND REVELATION

94. Content and Correlation of the Seal, Trumpet, and Bowl Judgments

	SEALS Opened by the Lamb	TRUMPETS Blown by seven angels	BOWLS Poured by seven angels
First	White horse: conquest	Hail and fire; ⅓ vegetation burned	Sores
Second	Red horse: war	Mountain of fire; ⅓ creatures in sea destroyed	Sea turned into blood; all marine life died
Third	Black horse: famine	Star called Wormwood fell; ⅓ fresh water poisoned	Fresh water turned into blood
Fourth	Pale horse: death	Partial darkness; ⅓ sun, moon, and stars darkened	Scorching sun burned men
	HIATUS: Last three trumpets announced as woes		
Fifth	Martyrs reassured	First woe: angel released locusts from Abyss	Darkness on the Beast's kingdom
Sixth	Great day of wrath; earthquake, signs in heaven	Second woe: four angels loosed at Euphrates; they slew ⅓ of the earth's population	Euphrates dried up; kings assembled at Armageddon for war
	Hiatus: Sealing of 144,000	**HIATUS:** Mystery of God to be concluded with the seventh trumpet	
Seventh	½ hour of silence; introduction of trumpets	Announcement of the Lord's victory	Severe earthquake and great hail

Adapted from Robert G. Gromacki, *New Testament Survey* (Grand Rapids: Baker Book House, 1974). Used by permission.

95. Contrasts between Genesis and Revelation

GENESIS	REVELATION
Rise of Satan (Ge 3:1-6)	Demise of Satan (Rev 20:10)
Satan's judgment pronounced (Ge 3:15)	Satan's judgment performed (Rev 20:2)
Presence of God removed (Ge 3:24)	Presence of God restored (Rev 21:3)
The curse received (Ge 3:17-19)	The curse removed (Rev 22:3)
Death enters natural creation (Ge3:19)	Death excluded from new creation (Rev 20:14; 21:4)
Pain and sorrow experienced (Ge 3:16-19)	Pain and sorrow excluded (Rev 21:4)
Entrance to Tree of Life barred (Ge 3:24)	Entrance to Tree of Life blessed (Rev 22:14)
Cycle of night and day (Ge 1:5)	No night, only light (Rev 21:25; 22:5)
First heaven and earth (Ge 1:1-2:3)	Final heaven and earth (Rev 21:1)
God clothes fallen man (Ge 3:21)	God clothes redeemed man (Rev 6:11; 7:9, 14)
God's face hidden (Ge 4:14)	God's face revealed (Rev 22:4)

96. Similarities in Genesis and Revelation

GENESIS	REVELATION
God's presence with man (Ge 3:8-9)	God's presence with man (Rev 21:3; 22:4)
Paradisiacal setting (Ge 2:8-15)	Paradisiacal setting (Rev 22:1-2)
Husband and wife (Ge 2:23-24)	Husband (Christ) and bride (Rev 21:2)
Tree of Life and river (Ge 2:10; 3:22)	Tree of Life and river (Rev 22:1-2)
Service of God (Ge 2:15)	Service of God (Rev 22:3)

147   **PART 11: DANIEL AND REVELATION**

97. Interpretations of Revelation

	REVELATION 1-3	REVELATION 4-19	REVELATION 20-22
Preterist	Historic churches	Symbolic of contemporary conditions	Symbolic of heaven and victory
Idealist	Historic churches	Symbolic of conflict of good and evil	Victory of good
Historicist	Historic churches	Symbolic of historical events: fall of Rome, Muhammadanism, papacy, Reformation	Final judgment; Millennium (?); eternal state
Futurist	Historic churches and/or seven stages of church history	Future tribulation; judgments concentrated on apostate church and Antichrist; coming of Christ	Millennial kingdom; judgment of wicked dead; eternal state

98. Theological Perspectives on Revelation

	REVELATION 1-3	REVELATION 4-19	REVELATION 20-22
Postmillennial	Historic churches	Generally historicist	Victory of Christianity over the world
Amillennial	Historic churches	Generally historicist	Coming of Christ; judgment; eternal state
Premillennial	Historic churches representative of historical states	Generally futurist	Literal millennial reign; judgment of Great White Throne; New Jerusalem
Apocalyptic	Historic churches	Generally preterist	Symbolic of heaven and victory

99. The Number Seven in Revelation

Seven Visions

1. Seven churches (1:9-3:22)
2. Seven seals (4:1-8:1)
3. Seven trumpets (8:2-11:19)
4. Seven symbolic figures (12:1-14:20)
5. Seven bowls (15:1-16:21)
6. Seven judgments (17:1-19:10)
7. Seven triumphs (19:11-22:5)

Seven Seals

1. White horse: conquest (6:1-2)
2. Red horse: war (6:3-4)
3. Black horse: famine (6:5-6)
4. Pale horse: death and hell (6:7-8)
5. Faithful martyrs: slain for Christ (6:9-11)
6. Great earthquake: planet shaken (6:12-7:17)
7. Seven trumpets: world on fire (8:1-6)

Seven Trumpets

1. Rain of fire: vegetation destroyed (8:7)
2. Fireball: oceans polluted (8:8-9)
3. Falling star: fresh waters polluted (8:10-11)
4. Sun darkened: air pollution (8:12-13)
   sun, moon and stars struck
5. Demonic plagues: suffering and torment (9:1-12)
6. Great army of the east: 200 million men (9:13-11:14)
7. Divine wrath: heaven opened (11:15-19)

Signature of the Sevens

1. Seven churches (1:4-20; 2-3)
2. Seven spirits (1:4; 3:1; 4:5; 5:6)
3. Seven candlesticks (1:12-20; 2:1)
4. Seven stars (1:16-20; 2:1; 3:1)
5. Seven lamps (4:5)
6. Seven seals (5:1-5)
7. Seven horns (5:6)
8. Seven eyes (5:6)
9. Seven angels (8:2-6)
10. Seven trumpets (8:2-6)
11. Seven thunders (10:3-4)
12. Seven thousand (11:13)
13. Seven heads (12:3; 13:1; 17:3-9)
14. Seven crowns (12:3)
15. Seven angels (15:1-8; 21:9)
16. Seven plagues (15:1-8; 21:9)
17. Seven bowls (15:7; 17:1; 21:9)
18. Seven mountains (17:9)
19. Seven kings (17:10-11)
20. Seven beatitudes (1:3; 14:13; 16:15; 19:9; 20:6; 22:7, 14)
21. Seven "I ams" of Christ (1:8, 11, 17-18; 21:6; 22:13, 16)

Seven Last Plagues: Seven Bowls

1. Upon the earth (16:2)	Grievous sores (16:2)
2. Upon the sea (16:3)	Oceans polluted (16:3)
3. Upon the rivers (16:4-7)	Fresh waters polluted (16:4)
4. Upon the sun 16:8-9)	Scorching heat (16:8-9)
5. Upon the throne of the Beast (16:10-11)	Darkness and pain (16:10-11)
6. Upon the river Euphrates (16:12-14)	Dried up to prepare way for the kings of the east (16:12-16)
7. Upon the air (16:17-21)	"It is done" (16:17 NASB) Earthquake and hail(16:17-21)

100. Revelation's Seal, Trumpet, and Bowl Judgments

	First	Second	Third	Fourth	Fifth	Sixth	Seventh
SEVEN SEALS (Rev 6)	Rider on white horse: the conquest	Rider on red horse: wars, threats, terrorism	Rider on black horse: famine, economic ruin	Rider on pale horse: death, hades	Martyred souls; more persecutions	Physical disturbances; earthquakes Silence	½ hour of silence
SEVEN TRUMPETS (Rev 8-9)	⅓ earth on fire ⅓ trees on fire All grass burned	⅓ sea turned into blood ⅓ ships sunk ⅓ fish dead	A falling star poisoned 1/3 rivers and springs	⅓ sun, moon, and stars darkened	Demonized locusts tortured men 5 months	⅓ mankind dead 200 million men from Asia went to Middle East	Earthquake: 7,000 died in Jerusalem
SEVEN BOWLS (Rev 16)	Boils on followers of Antichrist (Cancer? AIDS?)	All of sea turned into blood All fish dead	All rivers turned into blood	Sun scorched all mankind	Total darkness on earth	Euphrates dried up Asian kings assembled in Middle East for Armageddon	Earthquake collapsed all cities; Babylon cited Great hail

101. The Seven Bowls

	DESCRIPTION	REFERENCE IN REVELATION	OTHER REFERENCES
First Bowl	Ugly and painful sores broke out on the people who had the mark of the beast and worshiped his image.	16:2	Ex. 9:8-11; 2Ch 21:15
Second Bowl	The sea turned into blood, and every living thing in the sea died.	16:3	Ps 78:44
Third Bowl	The rivers and springs of water turned into blood.	16:4	Ps 105:29
Fourth Bowl	The sun was given power to scorch people with fire.	16:8	
Fifth Bowl	The throne of the Beast and his kingdom were plunged into darkness.	16:10	Ex 10:21-23
Sixth Bowl	The water of the great river Euphrates dried up.	16:12	Jer 51:36
Seventh Bowl	The greatest earthquake the world has ever known occurred. Huge hailstones that weighed 100 pounds each fell on men.	16:17-21	Jos 10:11; Isa 30:30; Eze 13:11

PART 11: DANIEL AND REVELATION

102. The Seven Churches of Revelation

	PRAISE	REBUKE	COMMAND	PUNISHMENT	REWARD	MEANING	SYMBOLISM
Ephesus	Good works, patience, exposed false apostles, hated the practice of the Nicolaitans	Forsook their first love	Remember the height from which you have fallen; return to your first love.	Removal of the candlestick	Overcomers will eat from the Tree of Life in the midst of the paradise of God.	Desired one	Apostolic church (A.D. 30-100)
Smyrna	Afflicted and poor, yet they were rich	No rebuke	Do not be afraid; be faithful to the point of death.		The faithful will be given the crown of life; overcomers will not be hurt by the second death.	Myrrh	Early church (100-312)
Pergamum	Remained true to the name of Christ; did not renounce their faith	Some held to the teaching of Balaam; yet others to the teaching of the Nicolaitans	Repent.	Christ will come and fight against them with the sword of his mouth.	Overcomers will eat of the hidden manna and will be given a white stone with a new name written on it.	Thoroughly married	Constantine (312-606)
Thyatira	Good deeds, love and faith, service and perseverance; doing more than they did at first	Toleration of Jezebel	Repent.	Jezebel will suffer intensely, along with those who commit adultery with her. Her children will be struck dead. God will repay each one according to his deeds.	Overcomers will be given authority over the nations and will rule with an iron scepter. They will also be given the morning star.	Continuous sacrifice	Roman Catholic Church (606-Tribulation)
Sardis	A few people had not soiled their clothes	Had reputation of being alive, but they were dead	Wake up! Strengthen what remains and is about to die; obey what you have received and heard. Repent.	Christ will come like a thief in the night to those who do not wake up.	Overcomers will be dressed in white, and their names will not be blotted out from the Book of Life. They will be recognized before angels.	Those escaping	The Reformation (1520-Tribulation)
Philadelphia	Kept the Word of God and did not deny his name	No rebuke	Hold on to what you have, so that no one will take your crown.		Overcomers will be made pillars in the temple of God. A new name will be given to them.	Brotherly love	Modern church–true (1750-Rapture)
Laodicea	No praise	Lukewarm; false sense of security; wretched, pitiful, poor, blind, and naked	Buy gold that is tried in the fire, white clothes to cover your shameful nakedness, and eye salve to heal your blindness. Invite Christ in.	Christ will spew them out of his mouth.	Overcomers will sit with Christ on his throne.	The people ruling	Modern church–false (1900-Tribulation)

103. The Sixth and Seventh Seals As Elaborated in the Trumpets and Bowls of Revelation

Seal	Trumpet	Bowl	Nature	Reference	Time
1			Conquest	Rev 6:2	
2			War	6:4	The
3			Famine	6:6	Present
4			Death	6:8	Age
5			Martyred souls in heaven	6:9	
A great earthquake				6:12; 8:5; 11:13; 16:18	
	1 ——— 1		Thunder and hail	6:14; 8:7	5 minutes (?) 30
			Sores on men (bowl)	16:2	5 minutes
	2 ——— 2		Sea turned into blood	8:8; 16:3	(with no. 2?) 30
	3 ——— 3		Water poisoned	6:13; 8:10; 16:4	5 minutes
	4 ——— 4		Sun, moon, and stars darkened	6:12; 8:12; 16:8	
The appearance of Christ			Total time of God's wrath so far	6:17; 14:14; 19:11	15 minutes (?)
	7		Silence in heaven	8:1	½ hour
			Flying woe-angel	8:13	5 minutes (?)
	5 ——— 5		Pain and war	9:3; 16:10	5 months
			Euphrates dried up	9:14; 16:12	
	6 ——— 6		The initial battle of Jerusalem	11:13; 14:20; 16:18	
	7 ——— 7				
The Battle of Armageddon				11:15; 16:17; 19:19	

Robert L. Thomas, *Revelation 1–7* (Chicago: Moody Press, 1992) and *Revelation 8–22* (Chicago: Moody Press, 1995), Wycliffe Exegetical Commentary.

PART 11: DANIEL AND REVELATION

104. The Seven Seals

	DESCRIPTION	REFERENCE IN REVELATION	OTHER REFERENCES
First Seal	Appearance of a white horse. The rider held a bow and was given a crown. He rode out as a conqueror bent on conquest.	Rev 6:1-2	cf. Rev 19:11-16
Second Seal	Appearance of a fiery red horse. The rider was given power to take peace from the earth and to make men slay each other.	Rev 6:3-4	Zec 1:8
Third Seal	Appearance of a black horse. The rider held a pair of scales in his hand.	Rev 6:5-6	Zec 6:2, 6; Isa 40:12
Fourth Seal	Appearance of a pale horse. The rider's name was death. He was followed by hades. They were given power over a fourth of the earth to kill by sword, famine and plague, and by wild beasts.	Rev 6:7-8	Zec 6:3; Rev 20:13; Isa 25:8; Jer 16:4
Fifth Seal	Souls of Christians martyrs under the altar questioned when they would be avenged. Each was given a white robe, and they were told to wait until the number of their fellow martyrs was complete.	Rev 6:9-11	Rev 20:4
Sixth Seal	A great earthquake. The sun turned black, and the moon turned blood red. The stars in the sky fell to earth, and the sky receded like a scroll. Every mountain and island was removed from its place. People hid in caves and mountains. They cried out to be hidden from the wrath of the Lamb.	Rev 6:12-17	Mt 27:54; Mt 28:2; Heb 12:27-29
Seventh Seal	Silence in heaven for about half an hour.	Rev 8:1	Hab 2:20; Zec 2:13

105. Theories of Literary Structures of Revelation

LITERARY CONSTRUCTION: 6:1-17; 8:1-9:21 and 11:15-19; 15:1-16:12 and 16:17-21:27

	Seals			Trumpets			Bowls			
	1-6	( )	7	1-6	( )	7	1-6	( )	7	( )
A parenthesis between sixth and seventh judgments in each series:		7:1-17			10:1-11:14			16:13-16		
A parenthesis between the trumpet judgments and the bowl judgments:						12:1-14:20				
A parenthesis between the bowl judgements and the description of the second coming of Jesus										17:1-19:10

SUGGESTED INTERRELATIONSHIPS OF THE SEALS, TRUMPETS, AND BOWLS

Seals
Trumpets
Bowls

Judgments are seen as occurring simultaneously, with repetition showing the intensification of the judgments.

Seals   Trumpets   Bowls

This consecutive arrangement envisions a total of twenty-one judgments.

This telescopic arrangement has the seventh seal introducing the trumpet judgments and being explained by it, and the seventh trumpet introduces the bowl judgments and is explained by it. So, the seven bowls equal the seventh trumpet, and the seven trumpets are the seventh seal.

Adapted from Robert G. Gromacki, *New Testament Survey* (Grand Rapids: Baker Book House, 1974). Used by permission.

EXPLANATION OF THE GREEK/MACCABEAN VIEW REGARDING THE DETAILS OF THE TEXT

The Hebrew text of Da 9:25 literally reads, "Know therefore and understand: from the time that the word went out to restore and rebuild Jerusalem until the time of an anointed prince, there shall be seven weeks; and for sixty-two weeks it shall be built again with streets and moat, but in a troubled time" (NRSV). Following this punctuation, the "word" that "goes out" is the prophetic word which "went out" to Jeremiah in 605 B.C. (Jer 25:1), which Daniel is reading in Da 9:2, for it had been sent from Jerusalem to the exiles in Babylon in 597 B.C. (Jer 29:1). Precisely 49 years (7 weeks) after Jeremiah received this word Cyrus the Great, whom Isaiah had predicted as "an anointed one of the LORD" (Isa 44:28-45:4), appeared as a Median overlord. In the Hebrew text there is no definite article before "anointed one", and in that the Hebrew text separates the "7x7" for the "62x7", they are treated separately here. The "restoration of Jerusalem, streets and moat, and in troubled times" begins in Cyrus's first year (538 B.C.; Ezr 1:1-2) and continues for 434 years (62 weeks) until another "anointed one", Aristobulus I (104-103 B.C.), is crowned as king of the newly established Maccabean kingdom. He is cut off within his first year of rule and is succeeded by his half brother Alexander Jannaeus (103-76 B.C.). Alexander appointed himself as high priest and thus incurred the wrath of the Judeans. A seven-year (1 week) struggle ensued, marked at the center (middle of the week) by a rebellion of the people in which "sacrifice was cut off" when Alexander was pelted by the crowds after entering the temple. In response, Alexander enlisted Greek mercenaries to slaughter 500 Judean elders. This time of abomination and desolation was followed by the decline of the kingdom until the Romans conquered the land in 64 B.C.

7 Weeks = 49 Years	62 Weeks = 434 Years	1 Week = 7 Years
From the promise to an anointed prince	*The era of restoring the city and sanctuary: from the return to Judea to the kingdom's restoration*	*Kingdom lost*
A "word goes out" from the prophet Jeremiah to the exiles (Da 9:2, 23a, 25a; Jer 25:1).	Cyrus begins the rebuilding of the city and sanctuary (Da 9:25c; Ezr 1:1-2).	
"An anointed prince" (Cyrus) appears as predicted (Da 9:25b, Isa 45:1).	104 B.C. The rebuilding is completed with the anointing of the Judean king Aristobulus I, who is "cut off" within a year (Da 9:26a).	94-88 B.C. "Abominations" against the "city and sanctuary" are committed by Alexander Jannaeus (Da 9:26b-27).

Reference for chart and explanation: Ronald W. Pierce, "Spiritual Failure, Postponement, and Daniel 9," *Trinity Journal*, n.s., 10, no. 2 (Fall 1989): 211-22.

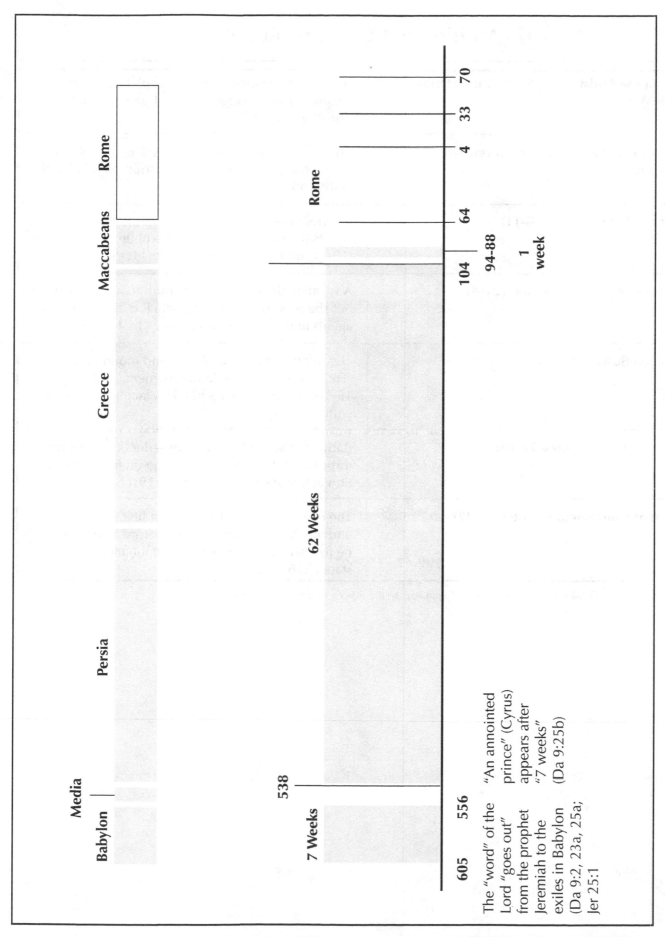

Chart 106—*Greek Maccabean Chronology of the Seventy Weeks (Da 9:24–27) (Cont.)*

Media

Babylon

Persia

Greece

Maccabeans

Rome

Rome

605   556

538

7 Weeks

62 Weeks

104   94-88   64   4   33   70

1 week

The "word" of the Lord "goes out" from the prophet Jeremiah to the exiles in Babylon (Da 9:2, 23a, 25a; Jer 25:1)

"An annointed prince" (Cyrus) appears after "7 weeks" (Da 9:25b)

PART 11: DANIEL AND REVELATION

107. Amillennial Chart of Revelation

Christ in the Midst of the Seven Lampstands (Rev 1-3)	Seven literal churches of Asia depict conditions in congregations throughout the church age until Christ's return (1:7).
The Vision of Heaven and the Seven Seals (Rev 4-8)	Christ rules from heaven now (5:5-6) until the Second Coming (6:16-17) with the triumphant church at the end of the age (7:16-17).
The Seven Trumpets (Rev 8-11)	A series of repeated judgments in the present age afflicts the wicked (8-9), but the church is protected (10-11) until the final judgment (11:15, 18).
The Persecuting Dragon (Rev 12-14)	A woman (the church) gives birth to a child (Christ), but she is persecuted by the dragon (Satan) and his agents until the Second Coming (14:14, 16).
The Seven Bowls (Rev 15-16)	The disappearance of islands and mountains (16:20) is seen as the final judgment, and chaps. 15-16 are events that will take place in connection with the judgment.
The Fall of Babylon (Rev 17-19)	Babylon (the world system of seduction) continues throughout the entire church age until its destruction at Christ's second coming (19:11-21).
The Great Consummation (Rev 20-22)	The present age (20:1-6) is not a literal 1,000 years, and this "millennium" occurs before chap. 19, to be followed by a general judgment and the eternal state (7:16-17).

Based on William Hendriksen, *More Than Conquerors* (Grand Rapids: Baker Book House, 1998), 16-19.

PART 12

Death and Afterlife

108. Eschatological Rewards at the Judgment Seat of Christ (1Co 3:14; 2Co 5:10)

	DESCRIPTION	BIBLICAL REFERENCE
Crown of Life	Martyr's crown for those who have suffered for Christ and have been "faithful unto death"	Jas 1:12; Rev 2:10
Crown of Glory	Elder/pastor's (shepherd's) crown for faithfully preaching and teaching the Word	1Pe 5:1, 4
Crown of Righteousness	A crown reserved for those who long for the coming of Christ has kept them prepared, leading holy lives while watching for his return	2Ti 4:8
Crown of Rejoicing	Special crown reserved for faithful witnesses of Christ whose testimony has been believed	1Th 2:19
Crown of Victory	An incorruptible crown given to those who discipline themselves to live a life consistent with their testimony	1Co 9:25-27

109. Biblical References to Heaven

Fifty-three Facts about Heaven	Scripture Reference
1. Heaven is being prepared by Christ himself.	Jn 14:3
2. Heaven is only for those who have been born again.	Jn 3:3
3. Heaven is described as a glorious city, likened to pure gold and clear glass.	Rev 21:11, 18
4. The name of this city is the New Jerusalem.	Rev 21:2
5. The city is in the shape of a cube; length, width, and height are equal.	Rev 21:16
6. The size of the city is 12,000 furlongs, roughly 1,400 miles long, wide, and high.	Rev 21:16
7. The city rests upon 12 layers of foundational stones; each layer is inlaid with a different precious gem.	Rev 21:19-20
8. Each foundation has the name of one of the 12 apostles on it.	Rev 21:14
9. The wall around the city is made of pure jasper.	Rev 21:18
10. The height of the wall is approximately 216 feet.	Rev 21:17
11. The wall has 12 gates, three on each of the four sides.	Rev 21:12
12. Each gate is made of solid pearl.	Rev 21:21
13. Each gate has the name of one of the 12 tribes of Israel on it.	Rev 21:12
14. An angel stands guard at each gate.	Rev 21:12
15. The gates will never be shut.	Rev 21:25
16. The palaces may possibly be made of ivory.	Ps 45:8
17. The River of Life is there to insure everlasting life.	Rev 22:1
18. The Tree of Life is there to insure abundant life.	Rev 2:7; 22:19
19. The Tree of Life will bear its fruit each month.	Rev 22:2
20. God's throne will occupy the central place.	Rev 4:2; 22:1
21. God's throne is likened to wheels of burning fire with an emerald rainbow canopy.	Da 7:9; Rev 4:3
22. God's throne is surrounded by 24 small thrones.	Rev 4:4
23. Near God's throne stands the brazen layer, described as "a sea of glass, clear as crystal."	Rev 4:6
24. Beside the throne are four special angels who worship God continually.	Rev 4:8
25. The golden altar is there, with bowls of incense.	Rev 5:8; 8:3; 9:13
26. The menorah, or seven-branched lampstand fixture, is there.	Rev 1:12; 4:5
27. The holy ark of God may be there.	Rev 11:19
28. The main street of the city is made of transparent gold.	Rev 21:21
29. The city will shine with and be enlightened by God's glory.	Jn 17:24; Ro 8:18; Rev 21:11, 23; 22:5
30. Heaven is a place of holiness.	Rev 21:27
31. Heaven is a place of beauty.	Ps 50:2
32. Heaven is a place of unity.	Eph 1:10
33. Heaven is a place of perfection.	1Co 13:10
34. Heaven is a place of joy.	Ps 16:11

Chart 109—*Biblical References to Heaven (Cont.)*

Fifty-three Facts about Heaven	Scripture Reference
35. Heaven is a place for all eternity.	Jn 3:15; Ps 23:6
36. There may be a tabernacle.	Rev 15:5; 21:3
37. There will be no temple.	Rev 21:22
38. There will be no sea.	Rev 21:1
39. There will be no tears.	Rev 7:17; 21:4
40. There will be no sickness.	Rev 22:2
41. There will be no pain.	Rev 21:4
42. There will be no death. Rev 21:4	Isa 25:8; 1Co 15:26;
43. There will be no more thirst or hunger.	Rev 7:16
44. There will be no more sin.	Rev 21:27
45. There will be no more judgment upon sin.	Rev 22:3
46. There will be no need for the sun or moon.	Rev 21:23
47. There will be no night.	Rev 21:25; 22:5
48. The city will be the Bridegroom's gift to the bride, Christ's church.	Rev 21:2, 10
49. Saved Israel will be there.	Heb 11:10, 16
50. The holy angels will be there.	Da 7:10; Heb 12:22; Rev 5:11
51. The Father will be there.	Da 7:9; Rev 4:2-3
52. The Son will be there.	Rev 5:6; 7:17
53. The Holy Spirit will be there.	Rev 14:13; 22:17

Seven Facts about Our Resurrected Bodies in Heaven

1. It will be a recognizable body.	Jn 21:7
2. It will be a body like Christ's body.	1Jn 3:2
3. It will be a body that permits eating.	Lk 24:41-43; Jn 21:12-13
4. It will be a body in which the spirit predominates.	1Co 15:44, 49
5. It will be a body unlimited by time, gravity, or space.	Lk 24:31
6. It will be an eternal body.	Jn 20:19, 26
7. It will be a glorious body.	Ro 8:18; 1Co 15:43

Three Activities in Heaven

1. Singing	Isa 44:23; Heb 2:12; Rev 14:3; 15:3
2. Serving	Rev 7:15; 22:3
3. Learning	1Co 13:9-10

110. Biblical References to Hell

Nine Facts about Hell	Scripture Reference
1. Hell will be a place of unquenchable fire.	Mt 3:12; 13:41-42; Mk 9:43
2. It will be a place of memory and remorse.	Lk 16:19-31
3. It will be a place of thirst.	Lk 16:24
4. It will be a place of misery and pain.	Rev 14:10-11
5. It will be a place of frustration and anger.	Mt 13:42; 24:51
6. It will be a place of separation.	Rev 2:11; 20:6, 15
7. It will be a place of undiluted divine wrath.	Hab 3:2; Rev 14:10
8. It was originally prepared for Satan and his hosts.	Mt 24:41
9. It will be an eternal place.	Da 12:2; Mt 25:46; Jude 7

111. The Future Judgments and Resurrections

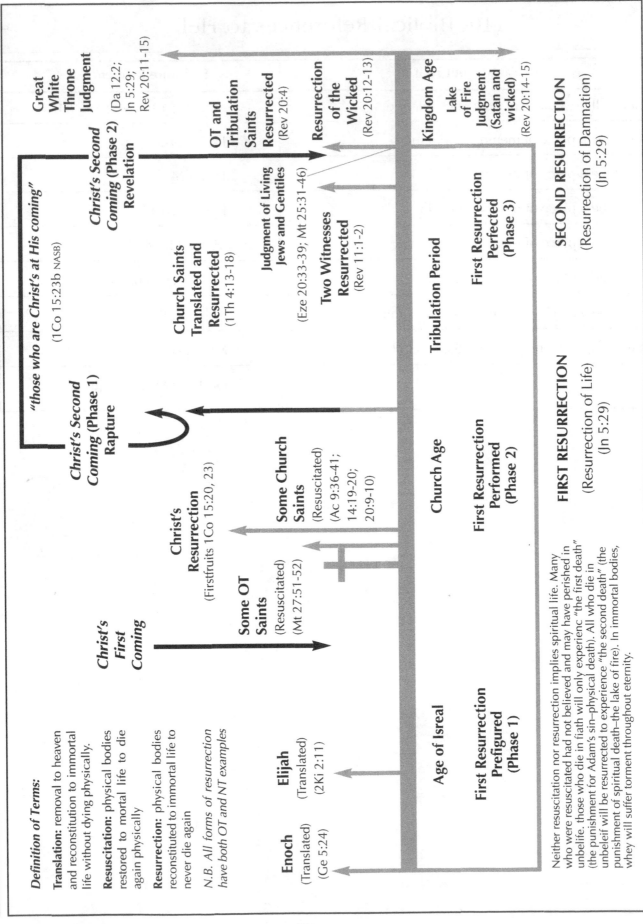

Definition of Terms:

Translation: removal to heaven and reconstitution to immortal life without dying physically.

Resuscitation: physical bodies restored to mortal life to die again physically

Resurrection: physical bodies reconstituted to immortal life to never die again

N.B. All forms of resurrection have both OT and NT examples

Enoch
(Translated)
(Ge 5:24)

Elijah
(Translated)
(2Ki 2:11)

Age of Isreal

First Resurrection Prefigured (Phase 1)

Christ's First Coming

Some OT Saints
(Resuscitated)
(Mt 27:51-52)

Christ's Resurrection
(Firstfruits 1Co 15:20, 23)

Some Church Saints
(Resuscitated)
(Ac 9:36-41; 14:19-20; 20:9-10)

Church Age

First Resurrection Performed (Phase 2)

"those who are Christ's at His coming"
(1Co 15:23b NASB)

Christ's Second Coming (Phase 1) Rapture

Church Saints Translated and Resurrected
(1Th 4:13-18)

Judgment of Living Jews and Gentiles
(Eze 20:33-39; Mt 25:31-46)

Two Witnesses Resurrected
(Rev 11:1-2)

Tribulation Period

FIRST RESURRECTION
(Resurrection of Life)
(Jn 5:29)

Christ's Second Coming (Phase 2) Revelation

OT and Tribulation Saints Resurrected (Rev 20:4)

First Resurrection Perfected (Phase 3)

Great White Throne Judgment
(Da 12:2; Jn 5:29; Rev 20:11-15)

Resurrection of the Wicked
(Rev 20:12-13)

Kingdom Age

Lake of Fire Judgment (Satan and wicked)
(Rev 20:14-15)

SECOND RESURRECTION
(Resurrection of Damnation)
(Jn 5:29)

Neither resuscitation nor resurrection implies spiritual life. Many who were resuscitated had not believed and may have perished in unbelief. those who die in fiath will only experienc "the first death" (the punishment for Adam's sin–physical death). All who die in unbelief will be resurrected to experience "the second death" (the punishment of spiritual death–the lake of fire). In immortal bodies, whey will suffer torment throughout eternity.

112. Perspectives on Annihilationism

Statement of View	All people are created immortal, but those continuing in sin are completely annihilated, that is, reduced to nonexistence.
Proponents	Arnobius, Edward Fudge, Clark H. Pinnock, Socinians, John R. W. Stott, John Wenham
Tenets	There is a literal hell. Not everyone will be saved. There is only one class of future existence. Those who are not saved will be eliminated or annihilated. They will simply cease to exist. No one deserves eternal, conscious suffering.

Arguments For	Arguments Against
That God would allow eternal torment of his creatures is inconsistent with his love.	This view places too much emphasis on the material aspect of man.
Cessation of existence is implied in certain terms applied to the destiny of the wicked, such as destruction (Mt 7:13; 10:28; 2Th 1:9) and perishing (Jn 3:16).	There is no lexicographical or exegetical evidence to support the contention that such terms mean annihilation. The way such terms are used in Scripture reveals that they cannot mean annihilation.
The eternal punishment spoken of in Mt 25:46 is just that, not everlasting but eternal.	In Mt 25:46, the existence of believers and that of unbelievers are set in parallel form. Both forms of existence are said to be eternal. The same word is used in both instances. If the passage speaks of everlasting life for the believer, it must also be speaking of everlasting punishment for the unbeliever. Otherwise there are two competing meanings of "eternal" in the same verse.
God alone has immortality (1Ti 1:17; 6:16).	God also confers immortality on holy angels and redeemed humanity. God alone has life and immortality in himself (Jn 5:26), but this does not mean that he has not conferred endless existence as a natural endowment to his rational creatures. Scripture presents death as a punishment for sin (Ge 2:17; Ro 5:12), rather than immortality as the reward for obedience.
Immortality is a special gift connected with redemption in Jesus Christ (Ro 2:7; 1Co 15:52-54; 2Ti 1:10).	Eternal life is a quality of life the wicked never experience. The term "eternal life" does not connote unending existence but refers to well-being in true fellowship with God (Jn 17:3).

113. Eternal Punishment

Description	Darkness (Mt 8:12)
	Weeping and gnashing of teeth (Mt 8:12; 13:50; 22:13; 24:51)
	Furnace of fire (Mt 13:50)
	Eternal fire (Mt 25:41)
	Unquenchable fire (Lk 3:17)
	Bottomless pit (Abyss) (Rev 9:1-11)
	Torment forever, no rest day or night (Rev 14:10-11)
	Lake of fire (Rev 19:20; 21:8)
	Blackest darkness (Jude 13)
Participants	Satan (Rev 20:10)
	The Beast and the False Prophet (Rev 20:10)
	Evil angels (2Pe 2:4)
	Humans (body and soul) are cast into everlasting punishment (Mt 5:30; 10:28; 18:9; Rev 20:15)
Effects	Separation from God and his glory (2Th 1:9)
	Different degrees of punishment (Mt 11:21-24; Lk 12:47-48)
	Final eternal state–no second chance (Isa 66:24; Mk 9:44-48; Mt 25:46; 2Th 1:9)

114. Compartmental Theory of the Afterlife

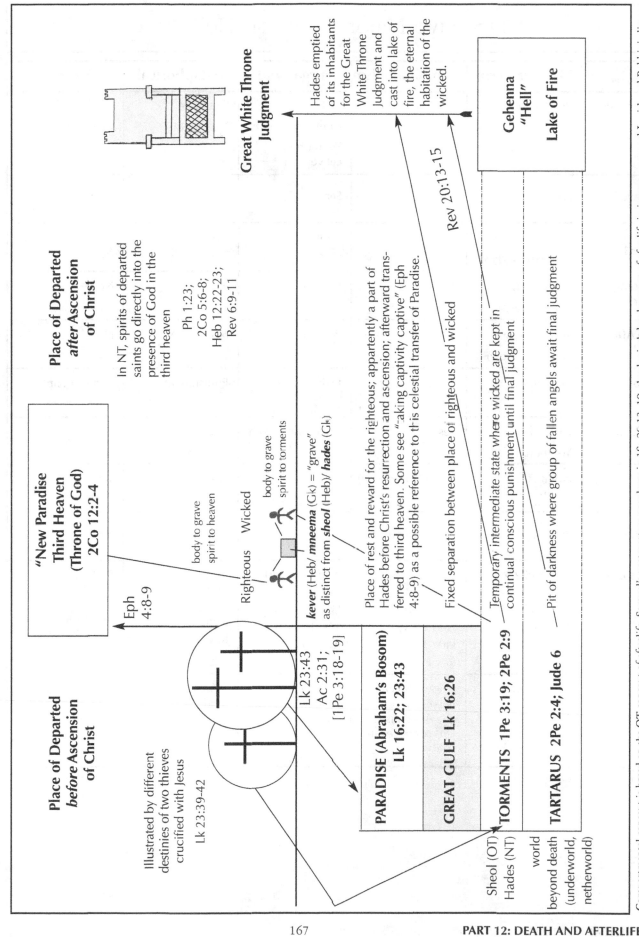

Place of Departed *before* Ascension of Christ

Illustrated by different destinies of two thieves crucified with Jesus

Lk 23:39-42

Eph 4:8-9

"New Paradise Third Heaven (Throne of God) 2Co 12:2-4

Place of Departed *after* Ascension of Christ

In NT, spirits of departed saints go directly into the presence of God in the third heaven

Ph 1:23;
2Co 5:6-8;
Heb 12:22-23;
Rev 6:9-11

Great White Throne Judgment

Hades emptied of its inhabitants for the Great White Throne Judgment and cast into lake of fire, the eternal habitation of the wicked.

Rev 20:13-15

Gehenna "Hell" Lake of Fire

Righteous   Wicked

body to grave
spirit to heaven

body to grave
spirit to torments

kever (Heb)/ *mneema* (Gk) = "grave" as distinct from *sheol* (Heb)/ *hades* (Gk)

Place of rest and reward for the righteous; apparently a part of Hades before Christ's resurrection and ascension; afterward transferred to third heaven. Some see "taking captivity captive" (Eph 4:8-9) as a possible reference to this celestial transfer of Paradise.

Fixed separation between place of righteous and wicked

Temporary intermediate state where wicked are kept in continual conscious punishment until final judgment

Pit of darkness where group of fallen angels await final judgment

Lk 23:43
Ac 2:31;
[1Pe 3:18-19]

PARADISE (Abraham's Bosom) Lk 16:22; 23:43

GREAT GULF   Lk 16:26

TORMENTS   1Pe 3:19; 2Pe 2:9

TARTARUS   2Pe 2:4; Jude 6

Sheol (OT)
Hades (NT)

world
beyond death
(underworld, netherworld)

PART 12: DEATH AND AFTERLIFE

Compartmental concept is based on the OT concept of afterlife. Samuel's postmortem prophecy in 1Sa 28:13, 19, theological development of afterlife in intertestamental Jewish and Rabbinic literature, and from a literal interpretation of Jesus' account of the "Rich Man & Lazarus" in Lk 16:19-31.

115. Five Major Views on Hell

	Universalism	Annihilationism	Purgatorial	Metaphorical	Literal
Alternate Names	Restorationism Reconciliationism	Conditionalism Conditional immortality	Catholic Further probation Postmortem conversion	Symbolic Nonliteral	Traditional Classical
Who is Saved?	All	Some	Some	Some	Some
Who is Tormented?	Some (old view) None (new view)	Some	Some	Some	Some
Literal, Bodily Suffering?	Yes (old view) No (new view)	No	Possible	No	No
Salvation After Suffering?	Yes (old view) N/A (new view)	No	Possible	No	No
Purpose of Suffering	Redemption	Punishment	Redemption	Punishment	Punishment
State fixed at death?	No (old view) Yes (new view)	Yes	No for those with venial sins	Yes	Yes
Hell Eternal?	No (it is nonexistent)	No (it is temporal)	?	Yes	Yes
Soul Eternal?	Yes	Believers only	Yes	Yes	Yes
Key Verses Cited	1Co 15:22 Jn 12:32 Php 2:10 1Ti 2:4	1Jn 4:8 Mt 10:28 2Pe 3:7 Heb 10:39 Jude 7 Rev 20:14b	2Mc 12:39-40 Mal 3:2-3 Lk 12:59 1Co 3:11-15 Jude 23	Jude 7, 14 (fire but dark) Mt 25:41 (spirit but pain) Rev 1:14	Lk 16:19-31 Jude 7 2Pe 2:9 Rev 14:9-11 Rev 20:10-15
Theological Persuasion	Liberals and Mormons	Jehovah's Witnesses, Seventh-day Adventists, and some "evangelicals"	Catholics and Eastern Orthodox	Evangelicals and moderates	Evangelicals only

Adapted from Griffith, *Eschatology*, 196.

PART 13

Comparative Eschatology

116. Similarities in Muslim, Jewish, and Christian Eschatology

	ISLAM	JUDAISM	CHRISTIANITY
Eschatological view of time	Linear	Linear	Linear
Purpose of Christ's coming	Defeat Antichrist, live 40 days, then die (He didn't die in A.D. 33 but has been in state of "suspended animation" since)	Defeat Armilus and Gentile nations, restore the kingdom of Israel, return of Jewish exiles, who rule in age of spiritual harmony	Rescue Israel, defeat Antichrist (Rev 19:11-21), judge the nations (Mt 25:31-46) and wicked in Israel (Eze 20:33-38), and rule over messianic kingdom (Mt 19:28; Rev 20:1-6)
Resurrection of the body	Yes	Yes	Yes (1Co 15:4-7, 12-23)
Destruction of present world	Yes (includes angels, earth will "spill out all its contents")	Yes (but excludes angels)	Yes (but excludes angels)
Signs preceding Judgment Day	Yes	Yes	Yes (Mt 24:4-28)
Judgment announced with the trumpet of an archangel	Yes ("siren" or "horn"; cf. Qur'an 56:15-56; cf. 36:51)	Yes (shofar will announce beginning of messianic era, gather the scattered exiles, and serve as a summons to the heavenly court on the Day of Judgment)	Yes (Mt 24:31; 1Th 4:16)
Who must experience death?	All people	All people	All people (except those living when Christ returns)
Basis for eternal life	Works (which result in attaining the mercy of Allah)	Works (by keeping God's commandments in the Torah)	Work of Christ (applied to sinner by grace through faith)
Levels of reward	Yes (seven levels)	Yes (three levels)	Yes (but degrees, not levels)
Hell as a place of eternal torment	Yes ("destruction by fire"; cf. Qur'an 56), in eight levels of torment (Sura 4:56; 14:49-50; 22:21; 74:27-29) eternally (47:15; 87:13)	Yes (Gehinnon, where bodies burn eternally in fiery pit)	Yes

Based on chart by Rick Griffith. Used by permission.

117. Differences in Muslim, Jewish, and Christian Eschatology

	ISLAM	JUDAISM	CHRISTIANITY
Nature of man	Basically good (Sura 7:23)	Good/bad (two inclinations within man)	Depraved (Ro 1:18-32; Eph 2:1-3)
"Purgatory" taught	Yes (called Barzakh)	No	No (evangelicals); yes (Catholics)
Assurance of salvation	Impossible in this life	Yes (but only for observant Jews)	Yes (1Jn 5:11-13), but some no (Col 1:23)
Nature of God as Judge	Allah is arbitrary	YHWH is just (Ge 18:25)	God is just (Ro 3:26)
Double predestination	Yes (Sura 35:8)	No	No (2Pe 3:9), but some yes (Ro 9:21-22)
Those experiencing the Tribulation	Believers of Allah hidden with the prophet, followed by "wind of destruction" which will kill all people	Whole world (Da 12:1), but Israel to be "delivered out of it" (Jer 30:7)	Various views: only unbelievers (pretrib); all, but believers only for 3 ½ years (midtrib); all, but believers protected throughout most or entire seven years (pre wrath and posttrib)
Christ will come again	Yes ("to break the cross and kill the swine" followed by an "eruption of a fire in Eden")	No, Messiah's (first) coming is yet future	Yes (Jn 14:3; Tit 2:13; Rev 22:20)
End-time signs	Major and minor signs reveal the last days have arrived (Sura 21:96; 27:82; 43:61) *Major Signs:* (1) Gross materialism ("beast of the earth": cf. Rev 13:11-18) (2) Women outnumber men (3) Muslims defeat Jews in battle; Muslims and Christians battle unbelievers together, then Muslims defeat Christians in battle *Minor Signs:* (1) Increase in bloodshed and war (2) Contraction of time (3) Religious knowledge decreases	*Ten signs* will accompany the Messianic "birth pangs" of the end times (Sanhedrin 97b). They are: (1) The world is either all righteous or guilty (2) Truth is in short supply (3) Inflation will soar (4) Israel begins to be repopulated (5) Wise people will be scarce (6) Jews will despair of redemption (7) The young will despise the old (8) Scholarship will be rejected (9) Piety will be held in disgust	*Beginning of birth pangs:* (1) Wars between nations (Mt 24:6-7a) (2) Famines and earthquakes (Mt 24:7b) (3) False christs (Mt 24:5) (4) Israel reestablished (Isa 11:11-12) *Birth pangs:* (1) Temple worship restored and abomination of desolation (Da 9:27; Mt 24:15; 2Thess 2:4; Rev 11:1-2) (2) Jews persecuted (Mt 24:9-10, 16-20) (3) False christs and prophets (Mt 24:11, 24) (4) Global preaching of kingdom (Mt 24:14)

Based on chart by Rick Griffith. Used by permission.

Chart 117—*Differences in Muslim, Jewish, and Christian Eschatology (Cont.)*

	ISLAM	JUDAISM	CHRISTIANITY
End-time signs (continued)	(4) Prevalence of the ungodly	(10) Jews will turn against Jews	(5) Celestial disturbances (Mt 24:29; Rev 6-19)
Result of end-time battle(s)	"Great Destruction," which destroys all but God, then a resurrection/re-creation	War of Gog and Magog, in which God defeats Gentiles and establishes Israel in its kingdom over all the earth	After Armageddon, Satan bound, believers enter Millennium; after Gog and Magog battle (Rev 20:7-9) destruction of cosmos (2Pe 3:10-13) and re-creation (Rev 21:1)
End-time rule	Gog and Magog led by Darius, the king of Persia (Sura 21:96)	King Messiah as God's regent rules over the earth until time of re-creation	Christ
Length of judgment	50,000 years (?)	World will exist for 6,000 years (2,000 Desolation; 2,000 Torah; 2,000 days of Messiah. The last 1,000 years [the Great Sabbath] will be a time of renewal [Sanhedrin 97a]	Eternal (Mk 9:43-48)
Temporal dwelling for dead	Most scholars say both good and evil with Allah, but some say "Alam Bazar" for all or for only the wicked	*She'ol* (place of departed spirits equivalent to the netherworld)	Christ's presence for Christians (2Co 5:8); hades for non-Christians (Lk 16:23; Rev 20:13)
Eternal dwelling for believers	*Janah* ("Paradise")	*Gan'eden* ("Heavenly Abode")	Heaven/New Jerusalem (Rev 21:2-3)
Nature of eternal life	*Mutashibir*—(sensual pleasure in sex with virgins [Sura 55:56], eating [Sura 56:15-22], and happiness [Sura 47])	Enjoying the radiance of the divine presence (Berakhot 17a)	Fellowship (Rev 21:3, 7; 22:4) Service (Rev 7:15; 22:3) Worship (Rev 5:9-12) Praise (Rev 19:1-6)
View of Israel	Eternally destroyed	Eternally restored (Jer 31:35-37)	Eternally restored (Jer 31:35-37)
Difficulty in understanding	Simple (unified views)	Complex (various views)	Complex (many views)

118. Christian versus Hindu Eschatology

One may not think the biblical view of eschatology presented in this study is really that unique until he compares it with the view of the future held by other religious groups. In particular, the eschatology of Hinduism provides the most striking contrast to Christianity.

	CHRISTIAN	HINDU
Concept of Time	Linear	Cyclical
View of History	History moves toward an end	History only recycles itself
Types of Deaths Per Person	Three: spiritual, physical, second	One: physical
Number of Physical Deaths Per Person	One: resurrection	Millions: reincarnation
Number of States of Departed Spirits	Two: heaven or hades	Two: rebirth or salvation from cycles (with Brahman or Macrocosm)
Soul's Origin	Created at birth	Gnostic/preexistent: only human after 8.4 million incarnations
Soul's Nature	Made in God's image	Emanation of supreme soul
Soul's Identity in Afterlife	Separate identity from God and other people	Indistinct identity (merged with the divine essence)
Fear of Death	None	Ever present
Resurrection	One per individual	None due to reincarnation
Accountability	High (believe and live now)	Low (just go through more cycles of life)
Judgment(s)	One based on faith	Millions based on works
Heaven's Nature	Worship of Creator	Gratification of sensual desires
Concept of Afterlife	More defined	Vague
Concept of Self (Soul)	Defined (sinful, separate)	Vague (ignorant, inseparate)
Results of These Concepts	Purpose, meaningfulness	Fatalism, meaninglessness

Adapted from Manish Jacob, "A Study of Hindu Eschatology in Comparison with Dispensational Eschatology" (unpublished research paper for the course TH 304 Eschatology, Singapore Bible College, May 1991).

119. Christian versus Buddhist Eschatology

POINTS IN COMMON	BUDDHISM	CHRISTIANITY
Immortality of the soul	Upheld	Upheld
Judgment after death	Yes (eighteen gates of hell must be passed to expose one's life deeds and determine destiny)	Yes (Heb 9:27)
Results of judgment	Punishment of eighteen types is applied to the part of the body responsible (liars/gossips have tongues cut out); some become animals (moderately bad people become rabbits, birds, or other carefree animals; really bad people become beasts of suffering who work hard, such as cows, donkeys, and certain types of dogs)	A general description of punishment applies to all in hell (fire, sulfur, pain, worms, etc.) but a specific type of sin is not attached to a specific part of the body
Who decides one's ultimate judgment—oneself or another?	Another (Buddha)	Another (God)
Effectiveness of rituals performed on behalf of one who dies	Ineffective ("No one has enough money to do the amount of good works required; therefore, works do not get one into heaven")	Ineffective
Hell as an eternal place of torment	Yes (but some say "no"?)	Yes

DIFFERENCES	BUDDHISM	CHRISTIANITY
Eschatological view of time	Circular ("in every ending is a corresponding beginning")	Linear
Afterlife	Reincarnation (thirty-one planes)	Resurrection
Resurrection of the body?	No (a different body is provided for the individual)	Yes (same body is glorified)
Nature of man	Basically good	Depraved
Source of truth and understanding	Meditation (self-motivation)	Scripture (God revealing himself to seekers motivated by him)
Concern for the future	Discouraged (it's a form of attachment to the world)	Encouraged (it exhorts holy living due to a certain future)
"Purgatory" taught	Yes, in a sense, as people have further opportunities in future lives to do good or bad	No
Basis of judgment	Karma: the impersonal natural law operating in accordance with our actions (if you do good, good will come to you now and in the future; if you do bad, bad will come to you now and in the future)	Faith in Christ

Chart 119—*Christian versus Buddhist Eschatology (Cont.)*

Assurance of salvation	Impossible in this life	God's will! (1Jn 5:11-13)
Source of judgment	Collective evil (the end of the world will occur when the moral attitude of society goes down to the lowest level)	God
Elements of destruction	Fire, water, and wind	Fire (water not an instrument of judgment since Ge 9)
Temporal dwelling for the believing	None	Christ's presence until resurrection
Eternal dwelling for the believing	Nirvana (the highest wisdom, contemplation of the ultimate, pure, unconditioned Truth)	New Heavens and New Earth (Heaven)
Eternal life given on basis of . . .	Works (the reduction of the three mental defiling factors: greed, hatred, and delusion)	Faith
Heaven	Not a place but an impermanent state of mind (or thirty-three heavens and twenty-eight subsidiary heavens?)	A permanent place
Hell	Not a place but a state of existence where one has a "subtle body" and mind which experiences "anxiety and distress"	A permanent place

Based on chart by Rick Griffith. Used by permission.

We want to hear from you. Please send your comments about this book to us in care of zreview@zondervan.com. Thank you.

GRAND RAPIDS, MICHIGAN 49530 USA

WWW.ZONDERVAN.COM